A Collection of Magical Secrets

A Collection of Magical Secrets,
Taken from Peter de Abano, Cornelius Agrippa and other
Famous Occult Philosophers

Being a translation of the final part of Wellcome MS4669 by
Paul Harry Barron from the original French dated 1796. The
initial parts of Wellcome MS4669 are *The Key of Solomon, King
of the Hebrews* and the *Universal Treatise of the Keys of Solomon*,
both of which are reproduced in *The Veritable Key of Solomon*
(Golden Hoard Press 2008, Llewellyn 2009) by Stephen
Skinner and David Rankine.

For further details of *The Veritable Key of Solomon*, which is
Book IV in the *Sourceworks of Ceremonial Magic* series by
Stephen Skinner and David Rankine, edited from rare classical
manuscripts see:
www.avaloniabooks.co.uk or www.goldenhoard.com

A selection of other books by Stephen Skinner & David Rankine on subjects related to the Western Esoteric Tradition include:

The Sourceworks of Ceremonial Magic Series
Practical Angel Magic of Dr John Dee's Enochian Tables (Volume I)
Keys to the Gateway of Magic (Volume II)
The Goetia of Dr Rudd (Volume III)
The Veritable Key of Solomon (Volume IV)

By Stephen Skinner
The Complete Magician's Tables
Guide to the Feng Shui Compass
Agrippa's Fourth Book of Occult Philosophy (edited)
Complete Enochian Dictionary (with Dr. Donald Laycock)
Terrestrial Astrology: Divination by Geomancy
Techniques of High Magic (with Francis King)
Magical Diaries of Aleister Crowley (edited)
Paracelsus' Archidoxes of Magic (edited)
Search for Abraxas (with Nevill Drury)
Aleister Crowley's Astrology (edited)
Geomancy in Theory and Practice
Oracle of Geomancy
Sacred Geometry

By David Rankine
Heka: Ancient Egyptian Magic
Climbing the Tree of Life
Becoming Magick
Crystals Healing & Folklore
Avalonia's Book of Chakras (with Sorita d'Este)
Circle of Fire (with Sorita d'Este)
Practical Elemental Magick (with Sorita d'Este)
Practical Planetary Magick (with Sorita d'Este)
The Guises of the Morrigan (with Sorita d'Este)
The Isles of the Many Gods (with Sorita d'Este)
Visions of the Cailleach (with Sorita d'Este)
Wicca Magickal Beginnings (with Sorita d'Este)

"In order to put this procedure into practice successfully, you should approach God and his Angels, as we have stated before, through leading a shrewd life and through prayer and you should know all their names."

A Collection of
Magical Secrets

Taken from Peter de Abano, Cornelius Agrippa and from
other Famous Occult Philosophers

and

A Treatise Of
Mixed Cabalah

Which comprises the Angelic Art
Taken From Hebrew Sages

Translated from Wellcome MS4669 by
Paul Harry Barron from the original French manuscript
dated 1796

With Introduction by
Stephen Skinner & David Rankine

Avalonia 2009

Published by Avalonia

BM Avalonia
London
WC1N 3XX
England, UK

www.avaloniabooks.co.uk

A COLLECTION OF MAGICAL SECRETS
Introduction by Stephen Skinner & David Rankine

ISBN (10)   1905297-20-3
ISBN (13)   978-1-905297-20-7

First Edition, February 2009

Design by Satori

Dedicated to Abraham Colorno (1530-1598)
translator of the earliest known *Key of Solomon*,
and engineer to Duke Alfonso d'Este

Acknowledgements

The illustrations from *Wellcome MS 4669* reproduced with
the kind permission of the Wellcome Trust, for which we are
duly grateful. Other illustrations by Jill Lake, thank you.
Our gratitude to Paul Harry Barron for his conscientious
translation of the original French manuscripts, his support and
encouragement for both Avalonia and Golden Hoard Press.
The image on the cover of this volume depicts the figure
which is drawn onto linen and used for wrapping the
pentacles as given in the *The Universal Treatise of the Keys of
Solomon*. For more information see *The Veritable Key of Solomon*
by Stephen Skinner & David Rankine.

CONTENTS

INTRODUCTION

Over the last thousand years there have been several distinct streams of Western magical practice. One of these is the Grimoires, which focus on preparation and complex procedures to produce effective communication and interaction with spiritual beings. To this category belong such major works as the *Key of Solomon*, the *Lemegeton* and the *Sworn Book of Honorius*, which have influenced many modern magical traditions and practices.[1]

Another stream includes rather simple rule of thumb procedures, which do not involve much preparation, and which might have been used by local village witches or cunning men. From the sixteenth century onwards these latter procedures were often to be found in works known as *Books of Secrets*, which focused on simple techniques that could be practiced by anybody rather than long and complex rites. Effectively such works made magic available to anybody who could read a book and gather simple ingredients, rather than the moneyed classes with their elaborate paraphernalia and expensive hand-copied grimoires.

The popularity of such Books of Secrets can be seen when you look at the number of editions published. The most famous of all of these books, *Secreti* by Alessio Piemontese was published in 104 editions in 9 European languages between 1555 and 1699. These books were amongst the early best-

---

[1] See e.g. *Wicca Magickal Beginnings*, d'Este & Rankine, Avalonia, 2008, for many such examples of the influence of these grimoires and others.

sellers, and contained a diverse spectrum of useful remedies from magical to medical, gardening to cosmetics and metalwork! Such books sold not only to the middle classes, but also at village fairs and wherever an audience could be found.

From the mid-seventeenth century scientists would start to repudiate Books of Secrets as propagating fake secrets and vulgarities with no basis in fact, and as purveying dubious folklore and esoterica which were challenged by the ongoing Scientific Revolution. Nevertheless in societies where a university education remained an expensive privilege, the Books of Secrets remained popular into the eighteenth century.

These two streams of practice, Grimoires and Books of Secrets, are sometimes found together in the same manuscript. It is common for the pages of a working grimoire to have been supplemented by its owner with other formulae that he had successfully used or picked up in his course of reading. These snippets are often drawn from books like Agrippa's *De Occulta Philosophia*, and the works ascribed to Albertus Magnus, and may be in a different handwriting. In the course of time these notes in the back of a grimoire were copied along with the grimoire as if they were part of it. Indeed the nineteenth century French pseudo-grimoires of black magic, such as the *Grimoire of Pope Honorius III*, the *Red Dragon* and *Grimorium Verum* are often full of such procedures.

It is as the result of such a practice that the contents of this present book finished up copied out in one of the manuscripts (Wellcome MS 4669) that we used as a source text for the *Veritable Key of Solomon*.[2] As such they provide us with an insight into the practices of a previous owner of that grimoire.

---

[2]*The Veritable Key of Solomon*, Skinner & Rankine, Golden Hoard, London, 2008.

The material is two collections entitled *A Collection of Magical Secrets* and *A Treatise of Mixed Cabalah*.

The *Key of Solomon* is the most significant of all the grimoires, being effectively the manual of practice which unlocks the other grimoires. The number of existing manuscript copies of the *Key of Solomon*, being over 140 dating between 1440-1825 CE, shows how much more common it was than any of the other grimoires, none of which can be found in more than half a dozen extant copies. The *Key of Solomon* describes all the necessary preparation, of the magician, place, and equipment, from robes to the magic circle to the appropriate prayers. Armed with this knowledge, which is often absent or only partially present in other grimoires, the magician could then perform the ceremonies other grimoires contained.

Of all the manuscripts of the *Key of Solomon*, Wellcome MS 4669, although one of the youngest with its 1796 copying date, stands out as one of the most significant, containing versions of two of the three families of *Key of Solomon* manuscripts. These are the Abraham Colorno Clavicule family and the Universal Treatise Family. The former contain the earliest known copies of the *Key of Solomon* manuscripts, and the latter much of the material subsequently found in the *Grimorium Verum*.

The subtitle of *A Collection of Magical Secrets* specifically mentions Peter de Abano and Cornelius Agrippa, two of the great luminaries of the Grimoire tradition, for whom there is absolutely no evidence of any connection to the material. De Abano's fourteenth century work the *Heptameron* (published posthumously in 1496) and Agrippa's sixteenth century *De Occulta Philosophia* (1533) were two of the defining works whose content would influence most of the subsequent grimoires. However it was not uncommon to use names from the past to give credibility and imply a much older provenance to younger or more questionable material.

The first part may initially appear to be collections of simple conjurations and remedies, preceding the second section focusing on practical Qabalah and angelic magic. However both sections contain interesting and unusual material which makes them stand out from other manuscripts, and shows that they are clearly more than just another collection of magical miscellany.

The operations found in *A Collection of Magical Secrets* are often referred to as *'experiments'*, and frequently contain a prayer or Psalm, and a basic written description of intent. The written items resemble simple charms rather than complex talismans, but are clearly meant to have a similar effect. Interestingly although these are commonly written on paper or parchment, in one instance the charm is written on a plate. The use of a plate is reminiscent of the spells written in a circular fashion on unglazed pottery in Hebrew, Aramaic or Mandaean found in the ancient Middle East.

Ancillary equipment like a feather, the blood of a dove, a green frog, or a strip of deerskin would all have been commonly available at the time. Herbs such as horehound, celandine, white or larch agaric, laurel, sage leaves, cyclamen or agrimony root, sesame, rosemary, honesty herb, olive, the common leek, honey and eggs are also used as they were in the Graeco-Egyptian rituals and charms seen in texts like the pre-Christian *Greek Magical Papyri* (2nd century BCE – 5th century CE). These items often do not have instructions to consecrate them, as are found in the Grimoires.

There are a large quantity of charms for regaining stolen or lost property, showing a wide range of sympathetic magic techniques such as dreaming, poppets, bread and sieves. The charms referred to as coming from Agrippa include a wider range of material. As well as many healing cantrips, there are a number of examples of how to gain a familiar spirit, plus the inevitable charms for winning in love and gambling.

Amongst the operations in the first part, is a conjuration of an angel, the Prince of the Thumb, onto the olive oil-anointed thumbnail of a virgin child or pregnant woman, along with associated practices. This practice has precedents dating back to at least the eleventh century CE, as seen in commentaries made by the Jewish scholar Rashi on *Sanhedrin 101*. Jewish manuscripts from the sixteenth-eighteenth centuries describe this practice, such as Codex Gaster 315 and 443, demonstrating that the practice was not forgotten or abandoned, and that it made its way into the French realms of practical (and often demonic) magic.

One aspect of these formulae is typical of Jewish magic. This is the naming of the person towards whom the spell is directed by specifying their name and then their mother's name, rather than that of their father. Another Jewish influence may be seen in the boat for transportation anywhere, which recalls the image in Oriental MS 14759, a version of *Sepher Mefteah Shelomoh* (the Hebrew version of the *Key of Solomon* in the British Library), of a boat being carried by two winged and horned demons.

Other formulae include the consecration of rings to Astaroth, Merazim and Lucibel (Lucifer). In the case of the former, the consecration is followed by the making of a sign in the earth with the ring to force the appearance of a spirit. This is particularly interesting because of the tales in which Astaroth steals King Solomon's ring, and with it assumes his magical power. It is also reflected in the use of the ring in some of the Solomonic texts, including the twelve rings in Wellcome MS 4670 published in the *Veritable Key of Solomon*. These examples also add a new dimension to the use of the magical ring.

Very few spirits are specifically named in these experiments, but when they are the style of magic reverts to a much more formal grimoire style of magic, where the need to know the correct names of the spirits is paramount. One example of this is the spirit Ebrion or Ebrionem (with Kaberion and Severion). When that spirit is mentioned, the name of his controlling solar angel, Carmelion, is also mentioned. This reinforces the traditional procedure seen in some texts of using a named angel to control a specific spirit. This particular procedure also involves the use of an image of the spirit.

Another named spirit, the Angel of Jupiter, is called Abor, who features as the spirit for treasures and riches as well as for honours and dignities. But this spirit talisman is just laid under the operator's head in order to get a prophetic dream answer. It is possible that this formula was inspired by the influential Arabic astrological grimoire the *Picatrix* as it relies on the preparation of metal talismans at the time of a specific astrological configuration:

> *"As soon as the Sign of Aquarius is in the Ascendant and the Moon is in the Sign of Cancer, during the Planetary Hour of Jupiter, make an image out of tin..."*

Another influence seen in a number of the operations in *A Collection of Magical Secrets* which stems from the *Picatrix* is the use of the Twenty-Eight Mansions of the Moon. These correspond to the path of the Moon through the twelve signs of the zodiac, and each Mansion corresponds to an arc just less than thirteen degrees in length. Each Mansion has an associated image and qualities, whereby it was believed that each Mansion was particularly appropriate for different types of magical operation.

The first part of *A Treatise of Mixed Cabalah* is a familiar description of the ten Sephiroth of the Tree of Life with their main qualities, i.e. name, divine name, archangel, order of angels, heaven, as well as which biblical character was ruled by the archangel. The specific details of the information strongly hints in places that this may have been drawn from either Sloane MS 3825 or Harley MS 6482, or a source or derivative of one of these manuscripts.[3] This is followed by a ritual sequence of prayer and actions for maintaining purity and leading a good life, performed over a series of days for increased knowledge of Cabalah or other revelations from the angels.

This text is reminiscent in its scope of the mnemonic grimoire the *Ars Notoria*, whose contents were aimed specifically at developing powers of memory and instant knowledge in the practitioner, and more particularly of a derivative form of it, the fourteenth century *Liber Visionum* of John the Monk. Although the content is very different, the practice of prayer to achieve revelations by angels to gain knowledge is a theme seen in such works, and can be seen here.

The second part of *A Treatise of Mixed Cabalah, Concerning Miscellaneous Cabalah 2nd Part,* is largely concerned with practical instructions for the construction, consecration and use of the seals. Of great interest here is that it also contains

---

[3] These manuscripts are both reproduced in Skinner & Rankine, *The Keys to the Gateway of Magic*, Golden Hoard, London, 2005.

detailed instructions for the use of wax pentacles in distance healing, with the aid of verses from Scripture. This is followed by sections on Properties of the Verses and Scriptures, and Verses for Illnesses & Infirmities.

The section on the properties of the Verses and Scriptures mirrors the type of use of the Psalms described in the medieval Jewish folk magic work *Sefer Shimmush Tehillim*, although some of the uses are different. In this manner we can see the continuation of a practice of magical use of the Psalms which can be dated back to at least the tenth century. Thus we see Psalm 72:7-8 and Psalm 92:10 being used here to gain favour as in the *Tehillim* (5 & 6), but Psalm 66 being used to praise God for the goods of the Earth (27), whereas in the *Tehillim* it is used for exorcism of evil spirits. This indicates it is not a straight copy, but rather the continuation of the tradition of magical use of the Psalms which is found throughout the Grimoire tradition.

The third part of *A Treatise of Mixed Cabalah* provides us with a technique for angelic dream incubation. The prayers and seals are given for the planetary angels, with a very concise and lucid set of instructions for their use. This practice of seeking prophetic answers from spiritual creatures through controlled dreaming has a long and venerable history, which can be traced back through the ancient Greek Asklepion dream sanctuaries to ancient Egyptian temples practising dream incubation.

Concerning Miscellaneous Cabalah Part Four is a system of divination based on 112 answers. This was a popular form of divination for some centuries, not relying on another person to provide the answers or be privy to private information. Thus precedents may be seen in the 100 answers of the *Golden Wheel of Fortune,* and in descendants in such works as *Napoleon's Book of Fate and Fortune.*

So this material, all bound together at the end of a *Key of Solomon,* is indeed a *Collection of Magical Secrets,* now made available in all its glory, some lesser and some greater, some transparent and some obscure. We hope you enjoy them and find value in their revelation.

Stephen Skinner & David Rankine
London
January 2009

Editors Notes:

We have included the Psalm references for the attributions in part two of *Concerning Miscellaneous Cabalah* for the benefit of the reader, as the Latin is in some instances corrupted and in other instances different words have been used to the standards in use today. We have preserved the integrity of the manuscript by reproducing the Latin as it was written.

The translation we have used is the Challoner revision of the Douay English translation of the Latin Vulgate *Book of Psalms.* The numeration is based on the Hebrew (Masoretic) manuscripts, and where this differs from the Greek (Septuagint) manuscripts, a second figure in brackets follows the first figure, e.g. 31(30) to indicate the Septuagint numbering.

A Collection of

Magical

Secrets

Magical Operations

For Difficult Objects

In Order To Discover A Wish

The evening before going to bed, kneel before an image of God and make the Sign of the Cross. As you hold the following names of the Angels in your left hand, recite this prayer with great devotion:

Prayer

"Oh venerable Divinity! Oh ineffable Trinity! Oh glorious Charity! I (Name), an unworthy sinner, I pray to thee, Oh Most high Creator of the Universe, who hast created all things, one after the other and who hast placed the boundaries of the sea, which cannot be passed and with kindness you have created

---

all creatures, while giving to human kind thy ineffable names, which thou hast wished to manifest for the salvation of their souls and bodies; with kindness, deign to listen to this prayer I am making to thee and show me through a holy vision, by means of your Angels, the person who has wished ... and the place where this person is to be found, such that I may see most clearly the person making the wish and the object wished for and the place, where it can currently be found and may this be done in a holy vision from thyself, my God and my Lord, Father, Son and Holy Spirit. Amen."

Then recite *"Our Father"* three times and *"Hail Mary"* three times and make the Sign of the Cross and then retire to bed and without fail, you should see the person making the wish and the object wished for in a dream.

It is important for the aforementioned prayer to be written on a piece of newly bought paper, bought expressly for this purpose, along with a pen and ink, which has never been used. After this, write the names of the following Angels on the same paper in this manner:

"Oh You Angels of God, Michael, Gabriel, Raphael, Uriel and Thobiel[4], be true messengers for me, be my guides and my directors in order to show me the thing, which I seek and may you endow me with He who must come to judge the living, the dead[5] and the Age through fire."

---

[4] Thobiel is an obscure reference, the father of Tobias, the central character in the *Book of Tobit*. Here he is being accorded angelic status and so may not be the same person. The other four archangels are the traditional elemental archangels, called in the Jewish ritual of *Kriat Shema al ha-Mitah*, for protecting the sleeper.

[5] This would traditionally be *"The Quick and the Dead"*, as seen in Acts 10:42, 2 Timothy 4:1 and 1 Peter 4:5.

When you go to bed, place this paper under your head, resting against your right cheek and after you have fallen asleep, you should see the thing you have asked for in your sleep.

IN ORDER TO MAKE A THIEF
GIVE BACK THE STOLEN ITEM

You need to take some blessed wax and with it, fashion a figurine or a statue of the person suspected of the theft. And write the name of this person on its forehead and then place this figurine into an anthill, while saying these words:

"In the name of Jesus Christ, thou art just, Oh Lord and thy judgment is just. Bestow thy virtue on this my ritual and be blessed, praised and glorified throughout all the Ages. So Mote It Be."

As soon as you have done this, it is assured, that the thief will never have any rest nor repose and will be forced to return the item he has taken without fail.

IN ORDER TO FIND STOLEN OBJECTS

First of all, you should recite these following Psalms:
"Audite hæc omnes gentes &c"
"Quam dilecta Tabernacula &c"
"Voce mea auribur percipe &c "[6]

---

[6] Psalms 49(48), 84(83) and the third Psalm seems to be a combination of words from Psalms 142(141) and 143(142): *Voce mea ad dominum clamavi*, and *Domine exaudi orationem meam, auribus percipe.*

Then write on a piece of virgin paper the aforementioned Psalms along with the following symbols, using a new pen and new ink, which have not yet been used. After this, go to bed and place this abovementioned paper under your head and in your sleep, you should see the thief and the place where he has placed the stolen object without fail.

Symbols:

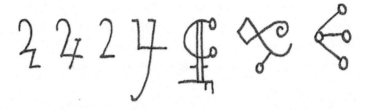

ANOTHER FOR FINDING STOLEN OBJECTS

With a new pen and with new ink, write the Seal or the Stamp mark given above on virgin paper and recite the prayer, as given below:

"Oh Father Almighty, who residest in the Heavens on the throne of thy Majesty and who can penetrate into the depths of the Abyss with thy look, by thy Holy Name Yod He Vau He, which is written with four letters, grant us through thy loving kindness the grace through which we will be able to find by virtue of this exorcism, the item, which has been stolen from us, Lah, Zah, Jah, and may the Spirits carry out this command through virtue of Thee, that the item, which we wish to find be shown to us. So mote It be."

Seal or Stamp mark:

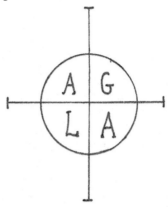

ANOTHER FOR STOLEN THINGS

Take a hot loaf of bread, stick three spindles into the bottom, in the way that you can see represented in the diagram below. You should place the loaf of bread on a small table in the middle of four lit candles and say these words:

"In the Name of the Living God, I conjure thee, oh thou loaf of bread, that if (Name of Person) has stolen ......, then this is the moment when I see thee move, but if he has not stolen it, then remainest thou still in thy place."

Then take out the spindle underneath with your thumb and index fingers and recite this verse from Psalm 69.

"Si vidisti furem currebar cum es, et cum adultero portionem tuam ponebar."

And here you should remember what your question is, repeating the same verse every time that you ask.

Diagram of the Loaf of bread with the candles:

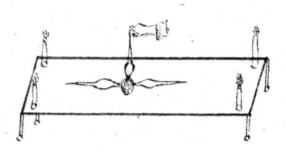

To Find A Stolen Item And To Know All Hidden Things

When you are determined in your wish to know any secret thing, you should choose a discreet person to assist you in this ritual. Then place a sieve or a strainer between the two points of a pair of shears and the two persons performing the ritual should place their middle fingers of the left hand under the ring of the shears, where the sieve is attached to the shears (as is shown in the diagram below). Hold it up in the air and state what it is you wish to know, while saying:

"Sieve, find out if it is so and so [Name] …. who has done such and such a thing."

Then pronounce the following mystical words:

"Dies Mies Jeschet, Benedoeffet, Dowima, Enitemaus."

If the named person is guilty, the sieve will turn, if not, then it will not turn. You should perform the ritual for each suspected person.

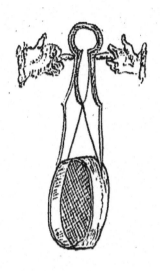

CHARM FOR LOVE

Write these characters with a new pen and with new ink on an earthenware plate:

Then wash it with blessed water or with very good brandy and give it to the person to drink and you should see some amazing effects, because she will be immediately struck with a burning love and this effect will last for as long as the person performing the ritual pleases.

ANOTHER CHARM FOR LOVE

During a day and during a time when the Moon is in an appropriate Sign,[7] write these names on a piece of virgin paper:

"Samuel, Fodiel, Beavel, Faraones."[8]

And when you have written them, hold this piece of paper in your hand and say:

"I conjure you, you Spirits named on this paper, by the true God, who has driven Beelzebub, your father, from Heaven, so that you may inflame (Name of Person), daughter of (Name of her Mother) with love for me and I oblige you to achieve this goal through the wisdom of Solomon,[9] by Heaven and by the Earth and by the Luminary of the World, by all that is seen in the sky and by all that is contained in the earth, so that (Name of Person), daughter of (Name of Person) will love me and will hold me in her affections above all other men in the world and may she be aflame with such a love for me, that may she have no

---

[7] I.e. Sign of the Zodiac. Presumably the sign of the desired woman, so that the conjunction of her sun sign with the moon will cause desire.

[8] The subsequent speech indicates these are the names of spirits fathered by Beelzebub.

[9] The use of the name of Solomon here as a word of control may indicate a reason why the material was bound with a Key of Solomon manuscript.

manner of rest until she has fulfilled my desire. Let this be done, let this be done. So Mote It Be."

As soon as you have done this, place the mentioned paper underneath her bed head and in no time at all, you will see something that will astound you, as this woman will not be able to live without you.

TO OBTAIN ANYTHING YOU
WISH FROM A PERSON

Take as much skin from a virgin deer as you have need of, so that you can make a belt 1-inch thick onto which you should attach the heart of an old dove during the Planetary Day and Hour of Venus. Then, on the abovementioned belt, write the following verses with the blood from the same dove and with a feather ripped from its right wing:

"Domine, exaudi orationem meam, auribur percipe obsecrationem tuam in veritate tua, exaudi me in tua justitia. Et non intres in judicium cum servo tuo, quia non justificabitur in conspectu tuo omnis vivens."[10]

After this, wrap this belt around the skin of your body, in such a way that the heart of the dove will be located above your heart. And then you may proceed and ask for what you wish. But, as you enter the house of the person, whom you are pursuing, you should once more recite the verses mentioned above and if you touch his flesh, you should get what you want from him.

---

[10] Psalm 143(142):1-2.

ANOTHER FOR THE SAME EFFECT

When the Sun is in the Sign of Gemini, take a chicken egg, in which you have made a hole and which you have emptied completely. And straight afterwards, you should fill it up with human blood and fit a stopper in it tightly, so that nothing can leak out. After this, place it under a brooding hen and leave it until the hen hits it with her beak. Only then should you take it and break it, and in it, you will find a body that is almost human. Take this body or figure, let it dry and then reduce it to powder, which you should give in a piece of food or in a drink to the person from whom you wish to obtain something, and who should not fail in granting you what you wish.

SECRETS
TAKEN FROM
AGRIPPA

TO MAKE YOURSELF LOVED

Take three leaves of sage and write, *"Sanctus, Sanctus, Sanctus Dominus"*[11] on them. After that, let them dry out and reduce them to a powder and with your own hands make the person, whom you wish to be loved by, swallow the powder.

TO MAKE A CHILD DRINK HIS MOTHER'S MILK

Take two silver coins that have been earned by a girl of the world,[12] bind them together and then tie them over the heart of the child and you should see results that are impossible to miss.

---

[11] "Holy, holy, holy, Lord."
[12] I.e. a prostitute.

To Make Yourself Loved

Take two bundles of Pentaphyllum[13] and allow them to dry. Reduce them to a powder and rub this powder into a piece of blank paper. When you have done this, write the name of the person along with your own and again reduce this paper to a powder and add some pulverised storax and magnet to this powder and give it to the person to swallow.

To Dispel Stormy Weather

Make a drawing of the World with a new pen, as in this diagram ⊕ . Then turn towards the sky and say these words: *"Ecce anna erga est."*

To Cure Toothache,
Headache Or Jaw-Ache

Make a plastercast the night before any of the festivals of the Virgin. Write these words on it along with these symbols:

Then place them on your head and say five *"Pater"*s and five *"Ave"*s.

---

[13] Probably Gynostemma Pentaphyllum or Ginseng, commonly used as an aphrodisiac.

This is the Plastercast

"Mentem sanctam spontaneam et honore et Deo et Patri Alpha et Omega[14], principum en finir, libera me a malo et peste, subitanea morte alque tremore et dolore capitis, dentis et

oculorum ☐☐☐☐ *salva me Domine."*

FOR A CONTINUAL FEVER

Write these words on the bottom of a white bowl, *"Caco, Carucet, Sanoriduce, Reputa, San Emanuel, paraclitur a Deo".* Then water down the writing with some wine and in the morning give it to the sick person to drink.

FOR A CRAMP

Take a laurel leaf and write these three names on it, *"Michael, Gabriel, Raphael".* Carry this leaf with you in a piece of clothing touching your skin, which should be attached at your right hand side.

---

[14] This is clearly derived or corrupted from the phrase honouring the legend of the Scilian Saint Agatha, *Mentem Sanctam Spontaneam Honorem Deo et Patriae Liberationem* – *"The Holy Mind, Spontaneous Honour to God and the Liberation of her Homeland."*

FOR TOOTHACHE

Paint a picture of a tooth on paper with a pen and say three "*Pater*"s and three "*Ave*"s. Then with the point of a knife, erase the picture while saying these words:

"*In the name of Melchior,[15] Gabriel and of Raphael*".

And continue to say this until the picture has been completely effaced.

WATER FOR WOUNDS AND TO REMOVE SPLINTERS, SUCH AS WOOD, LEAD, IRON AND OTHERS

Take a pound of brandy, three ounces of sciotri[16] oil and one and a half ounces of incense and one and a half of pulverised mastic. Mix all of these ingredients into the abovementioned brandy, which you should then place to one side. To use this mixture, soak the dressings and the compresses you are going to use on the painful area into it and in a few days, you should see some results.

---

[15] Melchior was the Magi who gave the gift of myrrh to Jesus, and myrrh was used for toothache, which may explain his inclusion here in this remedy.

[16] We have not been able to identify this.

To Make Yourself Loved

In the name of the person you wish to captivate, write these words on a slip of paper, *"Veni, Columba mea, coronaberi"*[17] and give that person the note, hidden in a little gift that you intend to give her.

To Stop A Nosebleed

Take some vinegar into which you have melted some verdigris. Boil this mixture and keep it for when you need to use it. Soak the dressings you place in your nose into this mixture.

To Remove Splinters
Without Using Any Iron

Take two lizards heads, crush them completely between two stones, so that they will be reduced to a paste. Then you should apply it to the affected part.

To Give Back Colour To Someone
Who Is As Jaundiced As Saffron

Take some Horehound, pound it and mix it with some very good quality wine and honey and then boil it. Take some in the morning and in the evening, boiling it again each time,

---

[17] *"Come my dove, you will be crowned."* This may well be drawn from the *Song of Solomon* 2:14 and 4:8.

which will brighten up the patient's appearance and will give him a better colour.

FOR HEADACHES

Mix some wine and some salt together and rub this mixture onto your forehead.

TO EXTRACT TEETH WITHOUT USING ANY IRON

Take some Ground Ivy and rub it onto the tooth that you wish to extract.

TO WHITEN YOUR TEETH

Render some Rosemary wood into charcoal and make a powder out of it. Put this onto a cloth and rub your teeth with it.

TO GIVE SOMEONE A BETTER MEMORY

Take some Agrimony root or a quantity of the herb called Sesame. Tie it to your right arm, or if you are a woman, to your left arm.

FOR TOOTHACHE

Say three times: "*Ut est amor cedis dolor*".

Against Weapons

Carry this sign ⚥ with these words, "*Clespida, signum vitæ*", which you should carry on your person and pronounce the words when you feel the need.

Perfect Quenching For Weapons

Take some green Leek leaves and make them sweat in a pot, in which they have been soaking and which has previously been heated up until the leaves were as red as a cherry.

To Gild Without Gold

Take some pieces of silver and boil them in the juice of Celandine. This will make them look like gold.

For Malaria And Other Fevers

Take an Orange, whose skin you should cut into small, thin slices, which you should then skewer onto a string, which should be suspended in a small jar filled with spring water. Then leave this out in the heat of the Sun until it starts to cook and simmer. Then, the next morning, while fasting, give some of the peel, which may have some nut shell in it, to the sick person, and he will recover.

To Give Vigour To The Stomach

In the morning and while fasting, take some powdered White Agaric[18] mixed with wine, enough to be able to cover the surface of an Ecu coin and you should then see some excellent results.

To Prevent Hair From Turning White

Grind some earthworms into a powder and mix them with some Olive oil, which you should rub onto your head frequently.

To Castrate Animals

Without Any Using Any Iron

Take some of the live glow-worms that fly around at night during the Summer. Grind them into a very fine powder and then give this powder to the animal in food or in drink and in a short time, his testicles will fall off.

To Prevent A Woman

From Becoming Pregnant,

When You Have Intercourse With Her.

Give her a small glass of wine to drink or some bouillon, into which you have put some iron rust.

---

[18] Polyporus officinalis, better known as Larch Agaric

ANOTHER FOR THE SAME EFFECT

If the woman holds some Cyclamen root in her hand ( )[19] while the man has intercourse with her, she will not become pregnant.

TO MAKE YOURSELF LOVED BY A WOMAN

Take one or two hairs from the head of this woman and from them, make a candle out of virgin wax and write your name in this wax and when you light it and you should get some results. When you see this woman, say *"Tuffro, Daffiel, Aspel"* in a low voice.

FOR THE SAME

Take a green frog from the meadows and place it into a pot of newly broken earth and bury this pot in an anthill. Three days afterwards, go and reclaim the pot and you should find only completely bare bones there. If you touch any person's skin with these bones, you will then achieve the desired effect.[20]

---

[19] Parentheses are in the text.

[20] This recipe seems to be taken from the one given in Scot's *Discoverie of Witchcraft* (1584), an earlier variant of which using toad bone is found in Agrippa's *De Occulta Philosophia* (1533).

For The Same With Powder

During the waxing of the Moon, gather some Valerian, on which you should write your name in your own blood watered down with rose water with an unused pen. Grind the plant into a powder, which you should throw at the person and you will see wonders.

To Make Love To A Woman
For A Long Time Without Ejaculating

For as long as you hold the herb they call Pepper between your teeth, you will not ejaculate.

To Be Appealing For Love

During the period that swallows have their young, take everything from a brood and place them all into a new earthen pot with a lid, alive. With the lid in place, put the pot with the birds into an oven, which is not hot enough to burn yourself but which is hot enough to let them slowly dry out, to the point where you can make a powder out of them. Take the pot out of the oven and take two of the young birds, which you should find a little singed and grind them into a powder, which you should prepare with ...[21] and you should give this as food to the person you desire and you will get some results.

---

[21] The ellipsis appears in the original text.

TO GET ANY INFORMATION
YOU WISH FROM A SPIRIT

Take the root of an Olive tree, burn it and make some powder from it and then mix it with some balm and with the oldest oil you have to make a black coloured paste from it. In a darkened room, use this paste to cover the palm of the hand of a virgin woman.[22] With a pen write on this hand, marking out the four Quarters of the World on it. Then draw four circles on the hand, namely, for the East a little towards to the little finger, for the South on the other on the Mount of the Moon, for the West on the other Mount of Venus and the last on the Mount of Jupiter to indicate the North. Then invoke a Spirit and say to him:

"O [Name][23] appear on this hand through this Pentacle and through this virginity; do as I command and I shall command you."

You should note the names of the Spirits belonging to one of these four circles or Pentacles.

---

[22] From the use of olive and the emphasis on virginity we can see that this is clearly derived from the Jewish practice of the Princes of the Thumb, where a demon was invoked onto the thumb of a virgin boy which had been coated with olive oil. This practice is seen later in this text.

[23] Name of Spirit

Properties Of The Herb Called Honesty[24]

If you cannot escape with any hidden treasure due to Spirits, obtain some Honesty, which needs to be completely pulled up with by its roots, while reciting the Psalm, *"Qui habitat in adjutorio &"*[25] and the seventy two verses or the names of God,[26] because Spirits like to look after this herb, especially in cold places and up on high mountains. You want to be sure that no wicked Spirit can harm you or prevent you from taking your hidden treasure.

Whoever carries a leaf of Honesty on his person, over the heart and fastened onto golden moiré silk, will be loved by everyone.

If you carry one of its seeds and other kinds of leaves in a red moiré silk bag, tied with a thread of red silk, over your heart, you will then acquire knowledge but when you remove it, you will revert to how you were before.

To Have A Familiar Spirit
Called Ebrion At Your Disposal

Begin by taking a plate of lead or silver on which you should engrave the image of the Spirit Ebrion[27] during the day

---

[24] Lunaria Annua, also known as the Money Plant.

[25] Psalm 91(90).

[26] This is a reference to the seventy-two names of the Shemhamphorash, derived from Exodus 14:19-21.

[27] It is interesting to note that Ebrion is the name of a seventh century Frankish mayor who was noted for his involvement in political power games, and so renowned for murder and infamy that he was named as an enemy of God in *Vita Sancti Leodegarii*.

of Monday and when the Moon is waxing. Onto this image, place the name of the Spirit on his forehead, along with this sign and towards the shoulders the symbol for the Sun and the name of his Angel, who is Carmelion,[28]

Then recite this conjuration.

"Conjuro vos, Angeli Solis, et nunc vos exorciso per nomen Summi Dei, quod est Alpha et Omega, ut per hoc nomen admirabile quod est <   >[29] et per ileum qui vos creavit et formavit et per signa quæ scripta sum in hoc lamina in vertute omnipotentia Creaturis et in nomine sublimia Dei, quod faciatis illum Ebrionem, cujus imago hæc est scripta cum nomine et signo ejus, in hanc laminam potentiam vestram intrare, et mihi obedire et in humana forma mihi apparere, et omnem voluntatem meam adimplere perfecte et veractier sine solo et fallacia, secundum suum posse in omnibus et quoticussique cum vocavero. Amen. Amen."

On the following day, when you have done this, write the name of the Advisor, which is Kaberion[30] along with his

---

[28] Sloane MS 3851 describes Carmelion as an angel of the Moon summoned in conjunction with the solar angel Scorax.

[29] The <> indicate a blank space in the original text.

[30] This name may be derived from the Greek Kabeiroi, the twin spirits who presided over the orgiastic dances at Samothrace in honour of the goddesses Hekate, Demeter and Persephone.

symbol, which is ✗ on the right thigh of the image we
mentioned before while reciting this conjuration:

> *"Conjuro te, O Spiritus Kaberion per omnia cœlestia terrestria
> et infernalia, et per Regnum Salomonis,[31] qui te subjugavit, et
> per omnia signia et sigilla sua, et per annulum ejus et per
> quatros elementa, quibus tolus mundus nutritur, et per
> serpentem exaltatum in deserto, quod de consilio domino tuo, ut
> te mihi exhibeas ad meum velle supplendo in omnibus
> secundum posse tuum quo desiro. Ei ceci tu le diras trios fois."*

Repeat this conjuration three times.

Then, on the same day, write the name of the other
Advisor, who is Severion, on the left thigh of the
aforementioned image and with this symbol ✠ and will
recite this conjuration:

> *"Exorciso te, Severion, et tibi impero per hoc nomen Elsytuh,
> quod nemo debet nominare nisi in periculo mortis vel arboris,
> quod sine mora aliqua domino tuo consilium præbeas, ut se
> mihi exhibeat socialem in omnibus quæ ab illo desideravero.
> Amen"*

Then recite this universal conjuration:

---

[31] Note the use of the name of King Solomon as a constraining word
of power again.

"Conjuro vos omnes, Storax[32], Carmelion, Kaberion, Severion, vos invoco, et vobis impero per Dominum quod catis sine mora ad Ebrionem, cujus sociatetem desidero, et per virtuter istorum nominum Crachy, Colphus & Erypus, et per Deum viventem, Deum verum, qui mundum creavit ex nihilo, et per omnea Angelos et Archangelos, et per omnia quæ in cœlo sum, et in terra, ut consitium Angelo Ebrioni præbeatir, et illum apparere faciatir in pulchra et humania forma, qui me certificet de omnibus, sine fallacia et dolo, que volo aut scire desidero. Amen. Amen. Fiat. Fiat. Fiat."

Then immediately after this, suffumigate the image with sweet smelling scents and when you wish to perform your ritual, recite this conjuration in a secret place, turned towards the East and with the plaque we have mentioned above in your right hand.

"O Ebrion, spiritus fulgentissime, cujus nomen et imago hic sculpta est, te invoco ut ad me venire digneris quotiescumque convocatur fueris, nec me fugas, sed te exhibeas mihi amicum libenter invocanti, ideo nunc invoco te per virtue Jod, Eh[33], Vav, Eh, et per virtidem summi Dei, quem omnes Legen Hebraïca, Caldæa, Græca, Arabia, Latina venerantus, et per regem tuum in cujus legione tu es et per regationem istorium quatuor Spirituum, quorum nomina in hac lamina scripta sum, et per signa eorum et per virtutem quam habes, quod statim et sinc mora venias in pulchra humana forma, mihi non nocens neque alio hanc laminam cui imago tua hærer in manibus suis habenti,

---

[32] Probably a corruption of Scorax, the solar angel associated with Carmelion.

[33] This has obviously been incorrectly transcribed and should be He in both instances.

apparear, sed cito venias ad me, et voluntatem meam perficias perfecte et sine mora. Amen. Amen. Fiat. Fiat."

And immediately, you should see the Spirit, to whom you should pose your questions and he will tell you everything that you asked him truthfully and without deception. And when you have finished, grant him license to depart in this manner:

"Vadun, Ebrion, ad locum tuum proprium pacifice et quiete et quandocumque te invocavero, mihi vel cuicumque invocanti istam laminam in manu habenti te exhibear et mihi vel illi obediar."

It is not necessary for your friends to cast any circle, as it is enough to have performed the conjurations above during the days we have mentioned.

To Make Any Spirit Familiar

Burn some olive tree root as you would charcoal and grind it into a very fine powder and mix with some very old olive oil, which should already have thickened with time and rendered into a balm like substance. Make a thick black coloured paste out of this balm, similar to printers ink and spread it in the shape of a square onto the palm of the left hand of a virgin child or a pregnant woman.[34] Then with a

---

[34] This is a repeat of the earlier example of the same, here showing its derivation from the Princes of the Thumb by stipulating a virgin child. The choice of a pregnant woman may be due to the belief that

stylus or a new pen, write the word "*East*" on the Mount of Mercury, making a little circle around it. Then write the word "*South*" on the Mount of the Moon, which you should also enclose with a circle in a similar way. On the Mount of Venus, write "*West*" and on the Mount of Jupiter, write "*North*", drawing a circle round each of them.

Then with a lit candle made of blessed wax, call and conjure any Spirit that you wish and he should appear to the person whose hand has been prepared in this way and she should see everything in her hand. By repeating this ritual often, you should also gradually see the same thing on the hand of this person, although you yourself may not be innocent. She should now be able to write on her hand but immediately afterwards, you should scrape off all of the coloured paste that has been smeared on her hand, including the circles as well as all the writing and place them onto a piece of virgin parchment in the shape of a circle. Or you could even apply a layer of veneer on the hand, so it looks like it had been prepared.

You should then be able to call the Spirits onto this paper, who should respond to you readily, and the virgin girl should be able to hear them by putting the paper to her ear. Then gradually, with some skill and being attentive, you, too, should be able to hear the Spirits and you should be able to hear them at any hour and without candles, day or night and obtain from them, whatever you want.

---

women may have greater psychic capacity and skill during pregnancy, or for the innocence of the life inside her.

To Receive A Reply From
The Spirit Of Jupiter In A Dream

The Angel of Jupiter is called Abor,[35] who is the Spirit for treasures and riches as well as for honours and dignities.

As soon as the Sign of Aquarius is in the Ascendant and the Moon is in the Sign of Cancer, during the Planetary Hour of Jupiter, make an image out of tin, purified in the name of Abor and on the forehead of the image write *"Abor"* and then in the evening during the first hour of the night, hang the image outside under the skies by its neck with a thread and immediately perform an exorcism so that Abor may enter into the image and imprint his characteristics onto it. The following morning, take the image down before sunrise and put it in a clean place and after you have done all this, repeat the process for three days and when you wish to find something out, place the image in question under your bed head and you should receive a reply appropriate to the question you asked from the Spirit in question.

To Gain Knowledge Of Everything
Through The Medium Of An Egg

Take an egg that has been laid on a Tuesday, then with two fingers rub it with some oil made from honey and as you turn toward the Sun, say:

---

[35] Abor was used in the ancient world as a shortened form of Aborras, a name of the Egyptian god Osiris. There is no evidence of a specific connection to this angel, although the function of treasures and honours would fit.

"I conjure thee, oh egg, by the God of Heaven and of Earth and of the Air, that thou showest to me, that which I ask (here you insert your question)".

Immediately afterwards, look through the egg and you should see what you wish, even if the egg is rotten.

A RING TO HEAL ALL DISABILITIES

In the hour of the sixth mansion of the Moon,[36] make a ring out of concave lead, into which you should place a piece of virgin paper on which these names are written: *"Abracalites, Abrazolit"*. Then as dawn breaks, fumigate it with dried human blood and recite this prayer:

"Domine Deus omnipotens Adonay, qui de cœlo abyssos vides, per quem omnia, qui hominem ad imaginem et similitudinem tuam fecisti, et spiritum vitæ in eo spirasti, quæso per nomen tuum Tetragrammaton ineffabile, ut comedas mihi, et aliis personia, quod quandocumque a me cum isto annulo tangantur infirmi N. N. ex infirmitate N. N. statim divino tuo auxilio convalescant, per omnes virtutes tuas quibus nos protegis, et propler gloriam sanctissimi nominis tui. Amen."

And when you wish to perform your ritual, say:

---

[36] The Sixth Mansion of the Moon is called Al-Han'ah and runs from 4° 17′ 10″ Gemini to 17° 8′ 36″ Gemini. This Mansion is for spelling adverse effects to medications, which is bizarre considering the purpose of the ring. Likewise the use of lead and dried blood must cause one to question this practice and consider it dubious in the extreme.

"Conjuro vos Abracalites Abrazalit, quorum in omnia sum huic annulo juncta, ut per Deum vivem, cui obedire tenemini, qui vos creavit et per nomen ejus Jehova, quod statim in hunc Dei famulum N. N. liberetis. Deo Christum Dominum nostrum. Amen."

TO HAVE A FAMILIAR SPIRIT

In the Second Mansion of the Moon,[37] have a silver ring made, into which you should have a topaz inlaid. Onto this,

engrave this symbol   , and on a piece of virgin paper, write the name of Astaroth and place this paper into the hollow of the bezel, while suffumigating with Amber, and this must be done in a clean place, while saying this prayer:

"O Domine Deus qui ex nihilo universa creasti, et constituisti nos super opera manuum tuarum, et omnia subjecisti sub pedibur nostis, oves et boves universes, insuper benedictum per omnia sæcula sæculorum. Amen. Amen."

Then, speak this conjuration:

"Astaroth, I conjure thee by the almighty name, who has given me the authority and who has appointed me to be in control over his handiworks and who has crowned me with glory and

---

[37] Called Al-Botein, and running from 12° 51′ 26″ Aries to 25° 42′ 52″ Aries. There may be some irony in the fact that this Mansion is associated with retaining captives.

honour, and by the terrible name of Agla, that when I make this sign in the earth with this ring, you will make a spirit appear immediately before me, who will carry out and obey all my wishes."[38]

And when you wish to make use of such a Spirit, make the sign with the abovementioned ring in the earth, after which you should place the ring back into a very clean place.

ANOTHER TO HAVE A FAMILIAR SPIRIT

If you wish to bind a Spirit during the day of Jupiter, you should construct a ring of the purest gold, on which you should find this Seal or Symbol engraved / And you should take this ring close to a dying man and place it in the man's mouth and when he is dead, take the ring out and return home with it. Three days afterwards, when you are all alone in your bedroom, get on your knees and recite three *"De Profundis"*[39] and suffumigate the ring with Rue and say:

"N.N. son of N.N. reply to me."

---

[38] As Astaroth is considered the Prince of the 8th Order of Demons, the Accusers, it is logical to assume that the spirit would come from this order.

[39] *De profundis* (literally *"from the depths"*) are the first words of the Latin translation of Psalm 130 (129), one of the seven Penitential Psalms: De profundis clamavi ad te Domine (*"From the depths, I cried to you, Lord!"*)

And straight away, he will respond to you and will be bound in this ring.

FOR LOVE

On a Thursday, Friday or Sunday, write these names with the blood of a white dove and with a red copper pen, newly bought in the name of the person, whom you desire:

"Rach, Sache, Raram, Amaam"

And then write the name of the woman and her mother on top of these names. Then with this paper, if you touch the bare flesh of the person, you should see a miracle.

TO HAVE A FAMILIAR SPIRIT

Take a completely black cat and a knife that has been intentionally made, making sure that has not been used to cut anything. Kill the cat with this knife and cut off its head. Then remove its brains and heart, after which you should make any kind of small Circle that you wish. Burn the brain and the heart of the cat in this Circle with some straw from rye grass. Gather up the ashes and when you wish to make a Spirit appear in the shape of a cat, take some charcoal made with oak wood, light it and put the abovementioned ashes onto it and a cat will immediately appear to you, whom you should be able to ask any question that you wish and whom you should be able to command.

TO RECEIVE A REPLY DURING SLEEP

On a Thursday or Wednesday, start a fast, remain chaste for three days and be free from all sin. During the 2nd Planetary Hour of the day, write this Symbol and its Intelligence, *"Assa"*, on a laurel leaf with some fresh ink made from rose water and with a newly acquired pen just sharpened with a new pocket knife. Place this leaf that you have just written on under your head when you go to sleep. Recite Psalm No.7 before getting into bed and rub your forehead immediately afterwards with a paste made from the oil of sweet almonds, which have been pressed without fire and with white poppy oil blended with powdered roses. Then, after having turned towards the East, say:

> *"Honorabilis Intelligentia Assa, tu qui Gloria et potestate a deo coronatur fuisti, supplio humiliter, ut huc amanter ad me venias, et invoco te ut nocte ista ad me placide venias, et clare, dum summum obumbraveris me, dicas et explices mihi responsum de hac interogatione mea N.N."*

Then go to bed without any more talking and sleep on your right-hand side with the aforementioned leaf under your head and near your ear, and without fail during your sleep in a dream you should be informed solely about the matter you wished to know.

To Stop Nosebleeds,

Women's Wounds And Hæmorrhages

Say:

"Azoropit, heal N.N. son of N.N. by the living God and may his blood be staunched"

Repeat this, saying *"Azoropit"* for a 2nd and 3rd time.

To Get Any Information

You Wish From A Familiar Spirit

Take a flask of clear glass during a calm day, fill it with clear water from a well and place the flask on a table facing a window. Then get a boy or a virgin girl to look through the belly of the flask and while he is looking in this manner, speak the following conjuration to him in a low voice and into his ear.[40]

"Rabiel adjiro te per illum qui ferit omnia, et per virginitatem istius pueri (vel puellæ) ut intres in hanc ampullam, et ostendas N.N."

Repeat this conjuration two or three times until the Spirit comes, because sometimes, he can be late arriving. Then in a low voice into the ear of the child, say:

---

[40] The practice of summoning spirits into water for divination, or hydromancy, has its roots in the ancient world, and is seen in some Renaissance Grimoire manuscripts, such as the seventeenth century Sloane MS 3824.

"Adjuro te, Puer (vel Puella) per Angelos et Archangelos, Thronos, Dominationes, Principes et Potestates, ut videas Spiritum rabielem in hac ampulla, qui tibi ostendat N.N."[41]

You should repeat this conjuration more than once until you get a result.

To Stem The Flow Of Blood

Say three times: *"May, Pax, Mux."*

To Brush Flies Away

Take some white Hellebore, crush it and mix some chalk into it. If you whitewash walls with this chalk, no fly will ever enter into a room after it has been whitewashed in this way.

Another For The Same Objective

Perfume the house with pastern laden leaves or with calabash leaves and throw some of this decoction onto the walls.

---

[41] These orders, Angels, Archangels, Thrones, Dominations, Principalities and Potestates, are the orders of angels belonging to the Moon, Mercury, Saturn, Jupiter, Venus and Mars respectively.

AGAINST RAIN

Take a new knife with a white hilt and make these symbols in the earth with the point:[42]

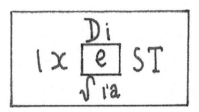

AGAINST FLEAS, LOUSE AND BEDBUGS

Fumigate yourself with a burned snake or scorpion and all fleas, louse and bedbugs will flee, as will flies. Even gall[43] and scurvy will go. I once knew a man, who killed snakes and scorpions with a simple touch.

You should also note that if a child is bathed in a bathtub, in which scorpions have been cooked, and if he is fumigated and scented as above, he will look young for the rest of his life.

TO MAKE A WOMAN GIVE IMMEDIATE BIRTH

You should perfume the woman's nether regions with pigeon excrement and continue to do this for some time, while making her sit over it.

---

[42] The white-handled knife was sometimes used interchangeably with the black-handled knife for such operations, as seen in e.g. Sloane MS 3847, one of the earliest known *Key of Solomon* manuscripts.
[43] This refers to fruits and nuts that have larvae infestations.

FOR LOVE

Take three hairs form the person you love and then take some wax running down a paschal candle and shape it into another small fat candle, like the shape of the hand's thumb. Put the three entwined hairs into this to be used as a wick and wrap each hair with a piece of colon and write these three names on the candle, *"Harton, Partonon, Arabiter"* along with the name of the person whom you desire. Then light the candle, but take care to ensure that it does not burn down completely.

ANOTHER

Take the person by the hand and as you are taking it, say these words in a low voice, so that she can't hear you: *"Cor Assabiel mulier."*[44]

TO WIN AT GAMES

On a day of Wednesday, take the card of the King of Coins from the Tarot Deck[45] and write these symbols on the back of the card with the blood of a weasel:

---

[44] This name may be derived from Assaba, one of the Dukes serving Gediel by day in the Theurgia Goetia.

[45] The use of the Tarot is interesting, particularly with the appropriate symbolic wealth associations of the card.

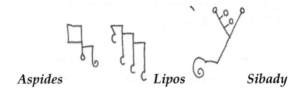

Aspides   *Lipos*   *Sibady*

Then fold the card in question, wrapping it in a piece of golden green moiré silk and carry it on your person.

FOR GAMES

During a day of Sunday during the waxing of the Moon, write these symbols on white virgin paper with the blood of a male crow:

Then carry this paper on you.

FOR LOVE

Stare a person in the eye and while looking at them like this, utter these words in a low voice, *"Libaresol, Onpiqua, Lesoref"* and, *"Ange"*.

ANOTHER

On a day of Friday, at sunrise, write this word with these symbols on your right hand with the blood of a dove, *"Anariel*

" and if you touch the bare flesh of the person you should get some effective results.

TO BE INVISIBLE

Take a black cockerel and cut off its head from its neck with three blows and say, *"I kill you in the name of the Devil."* When you have done that, take 15 or 20 black bean pods and place them into the body of the cockerel.[46] Then close up the body and place the body so prepared, into a hole made in a garden or any other place where beans can grow in the soil, while saying: *"Here, oh Devil, a cockerel worthy of you."*

I hear that the beans that spring from the body of the cockerel will have the ability to render a person carrying one of these beans in his mouth invisible and that nobody will be able to see, sense or hear him in any way whatsoever, nor touch him or sense him by any other human means.

Then cover up the body of the cockerel with earth and from it, a plant will spring forth, which you should allow to grow and mature. When it is mature, take a virgin child along with you and make him harvest the beans one after the other. As soon as they are picked, place them into your hands and

---

[46] The use of beans in invisibility spells can be found in a number of manuscripts from the fifteenth century Greek text Harley MS 5596 through to the nineteenth century *Grimorium Verum*. See the excellent article *"From the Ring of Gyges to the Black Cat Bone: A Historical Survey of the Invisibility Spells"* by Ioannis Marathakis at www.hermetics.org/invisibilitas.html for a very good study of this subject.

test them, one by one, by placing them in the child's mouth to discover which one makes the child invisible. And when you find the one that does, keep it. But test all of them at the same time that they are picked.

TO SEE A SPIRIT ON YOUR HAND

Make a virgin child kneel and make him hold a lit church candle that has been blessed, between the middle finger and the ring finger then say:

"Oh you pure Angels! Oh you holy Angels, who have come from the Heavens and who have descended upon the Earth, I pray to you through your purity and through the virginity of this child, that you appear on this hand and that upon it, you show me (   ), which I desire to know."

Then you should say one *"Pater"* and one *"Ave"*. And if nothing materialises, repeat the same prayer again up to nine times, but they usually appear after the third time.

FOR LOVE

On a day of Friday early in the morning and when the Moon is in the sign of Cancer, write your name along with that of the person you want to be loved by onto a laurel leaf with some saffron mixed with twice as much rose water. Write these names, too: *"Rex, Flex, Flon, Lacom."*

Then place this leaf into the earth in some place where the person will have to pass and walk over it and you should leave it there for four days, after which, collect it and carry it on your person, while making a conjuration to it, appropriate and adapted to the person in question.

TO HEAL A SICK MAN FROM THE EVILS MENTIONED IN THE FOLLOWING CIRCLE, WHICH HAVE EITHER BEEN CAUSED BY SORCERY OR BY NATURAL CAUSES

Draw this Circle on a white glazed plate with the words written inside it and with the names written on the periphery. Then, scrape the drawn circle and the inscribed words off the plate and mix them with a little water, and give this water to the sick person to drink for three mornings in a row.

To Be Transported To Any Place That You Wish To Go In A Boat Or Vessel

Get yourself a sword or a sabre which has been used to kill a man and with its point, draw the boat shown on the facing page, onto the earth or onto a piece of wood, which must be big enough for you to be able to place your two feet into. Then make the Sign of the Cross and enter into the mentioned boat with both feet and say these words:

> *"O vos invoco, venite, venite et statim quo volo me ducite, et sine iæsiom corporis et animæ, invoco Angelos gloriosos quocumque libet littera scripta est in nave ista nominatos; Gabrion, Sisoy, Gabzav, Pelvm, Gadym, Meos, Artos, Salixos, Gulas, Alabxatas. "*

The boat will then immediately appear and will transport you to any place that you wish to go and you do not need fear any evil, as there is no danger.

The Philosopher who made this procedure known for us, assures us that the Angels that have been invoked here are good Spirits of God, who give joy and make all things that we wish to know in the present or future known to us.

Here is the Boat:

TO RECEIVE A REPLY FROM A SPIRIT[47]

Take a virgin boy or a virgin girl or a seven or eight month pregnant woman and make her graze her right hand thumb nail and then rub olive oil into this nail, making the nail face the sun and while holding the hand of that person in your hand in, say these words in a very low voice:

"Huriel,[48] Seraphim, Potestates, Anglata, Calim Cala. Be thou welcome, be thou welcome, be thou welcome. Take the stool and place it on the floor. Take the Book, which God gave to Moses, open it and place thy hand upon it and swear an oath that thou wilt tell me the truth of anything that I ask of thee, by the four words God that uttered from his own mouth, "Heu, Zatti, Zati, Habatho" and by the four Heavens, where thou dwellest and by the virginity, which is placed before thee, Huriel, show thyself to this pregnant woman (   )[49] and I will then permit thee to

---

[47] This is the method known as the Princes of the Thumb.

[48] Huriel is an angel mentioned in the 13th century grimoire *Liber Juratus*.

[49] Parentheses are in the text, presumably for the name of the woman to be inserted.

return to the place, which has been predestined to thee. Fiat.
Fiat. Fiat."

You should repeat this several times until the Spirit appears, who normally appears in the form of a child dressed in white, with his hand holding a book. When he appears, say to him:

"Huriel, I command thee by the four words which God uttered from his own mouth, Heu, Zatti, Zata, Habatho and by the four Heavens, where thou dwellest and by the virginity that I present before thee, Huriel, that thou showest and makest these ( ) ( )[50] be seen and I will then permit thee to return to the place predestined to thee. Fiat. Fiat. Fiat."

You should continue with this conjuration until the person you are employing sees what is being asked for clearly on her nail, and as soon as this happens, say:

"Oh Huriel, depart now to the place predestined to thee and hold thyself ready to swiftly return when thou art called again."

It should be noted that if you do this ritual on a day of Sunday during the first rays of daylight, the Spirit should come quickly and without too much difficulty.

---

[50] The magician would insert the vision required here.

SECOND METHOD TO HAVE A REPLY
FROM THE SPIRIT HURIEL

This Huriel that we have talked about above, is so familiar and friendly, that he always comes, no matter how you call him, and the speed with which he comes to you, is in accordance with how much you honour him.

If you wished, therefore, to make him appear in a flask full of water, you only need take a crystal flask, as shown in this diagram and fill it with very clear water. You should expose the flask of water to the sun, while standing it on a small and really clean table, covered with a really white cloth, between two silver or silver-plated exceptionally clean and gleaming candle holders, each of which should be holding a candle made of new and extremely white wax.

Immediately light these candles and make the person, whom you are employing, kneel before the flask. This person needs to be a virgin, boy or girl, or a pregnant woman, as has been stated in the previous paragraph and you should also kneel behind this person and hold your right hand over her head, while saying the following words:

"Huriel, Seraphim, Potestates, Anglati, Anglata, Calim, Cala, be thou welcome, be thou welcome, be thou welcome. Take a stool and take the Book, which God gave to Moses, open it and place your hand upon it and swear an oath that thou wilt tell me truth of everything that I ask of thee, by the four Words that God uttered from his own mouth, "Heu, zatti, Zata, Habatho" and by the four Heavens, where thou dwellest and by the virginity that I present before thee, Huriel, show thyself to (   )

and then I will permit thee to return to the place predestined to thee. Fiat. Fiat. Fiat."

Continue with the same conjuration until he appears in the flask and he should do so even more quickly.[51] Your clothes, as well as your body, should be even cleaner and tidier and you should have washed and perfumed yourself with Aloe wood incense beforehand. You should even have made sure to have placed a new pot with lit charcoal onto the little table where you should cast your incense and Aloe wood. In this way, he is duty bound to take on a shape swiftly and to appear immediately.   And when the person that you are employing sees the Spirit in the shape of a child dressed in white and holding a book in his hand in the flask, say:

"Huriel, I command thee to let this child see (   ) (   ) by the four words that God uttered with his own mouth, "Heu, Zatti, Zata, Habatho" and by the four Heavens where thou dwellest and by the virginity, that I present before thee, Huriel, show and let this child see (   ) (   ) and I will then permit thee to return to the place predestined to thee. Fiat. Fiat. Fiat."

If the Spirit delays in showing you the thing you have asked for, then you should continue to repeat this last conjuration until he has obeyed.

When you have obtained [the response to] your question, grant the spirit license to depart in the way that has been given above.

---

[51] Another example of water being used as the medium for a spirit to manifest in.

OBSERVATIONS ON

THE TWO PRECEDING PROCEDURES

Note, that you can also make the Spirit of Uriel[52] appear in a mirror, in a spring of sparkling water, in a crystal ball or even in a piece of polished stone, provided that all these bodies have been bathed in sunlight and that they can reflect the image that is being presented to them. As for the method you should follow, it is the same one as for the two preceding procedures.

TO HOLD THE SPIRIT MERAZIM IN A RING, WHO RULES OVER SCIENCES

On a day of Wednesday, Thursday, Friday or Sunday, during first hour of these days, have a ring made from gold and in the hollow of the bezel, engrave this name, "Merazim".[53] Then fill in the lettered hollow with Dragon's Blood and on top of it, fit a crystal plate, so that you can see through to the name we have mentioned. Then sprinkle the ring with rose water and perfume it with sweet-smelling scents. After you have done this, place the ring in some silken material and safeguard it in a very clean place, to be used according to your needs.

---

[52] Uriel would more normally be referred to as an archangel. He is associated with the science of astrology, and hence is ideal for divination.

[53] This could be derived from the Hebrew *Mezarim*, a term which may refer to the constellations of Ursa Major or Ursa Minor.

As you need to be very clean before making this ring or band, you should have made sure that you have bathed and washed yourself thoroughly and clothed yourself in white clothes made from washed white linen.

And when you wish to speak with the Spirit we have mentioned above, make sure that you are prepared and you have armed yourself with all the necessary things, according to what the Art prescribes. And when you have cast a circle in the usual manner, the person conducting the ritual should place himself in the centre and he should invoke the Spirit and conjure him up gently, as the Art instructs. This should make him appear but if he does not come, the person conducting the ritual should repeat the conjuration until he does come and has done and answered what you have asked of him. After this, you should grant him license to depart in the accustomed manner.

ANOTHER TO HAVE A FAMILIAR SPIRIT

Approach a sick man who is dying by yourself and alone and say these words into his right ear:

"Deus Pater Alba, vel Abba, Melcho, Ysquibor et ad meam voluntatum constringam te omnibus horis."

And into his left ear say:

"Tetragrammaton cum hæc septia, phecton, vel Amech, Fenesiethia, Fathon in med servitio, et utilitate, et sine læsione aliqua protegat."

After that, place your right hand upon his head and say to him:

"(   )[54], *conjuro te per supradicta nomina et per ipsum Deum, qui cœlorum continir Thronos, et abyssos intuctur, qui est Rex regum et Dominus dominantium, qui montres ponderat, terram quoque palmo suo concludit, qui fecit Angelos, Spiritus et Ministros suos flammam ignis, qui producit ventos de thesauris suia; qui percussit primogentor ab homine usque ad pecur; qui divisit lucem a tenebris; qui facit mirabilia magna solus, ut in quacumque hora diei vel noctis te invocavero sive in domo, sive extra dominum, sive in quocumque alio loco, ad me venire debeas sine aliquot furore aut terrare, non incutiens metum, sed quiete et pacifice ac benigite venias, et de quacumque re te interregavero mihi diras veritatem aperte et sine fallatia absque dilatione pro posse tuo ministrare obedias, et ego tibi promitto in verbo veritatis et infide Dei illum exorare ut tibi comedat omnem gratiam quam tibi ab illo sperare fas est. Amen."*

Then say some prayers to God for the sdeceased, in accordance with the promise you made to him.

DR. ETIENNE'S PROCEDURE

FOR SPEAKING WITH A SPIRIT

During the waxing of the Moon and during its first Hour, take the figurine of a woman standing up and holding a young girl in her arms. The figurine should be made by some skilled artist or even by yourself out of silver or tin. Make sure that before you make this figurine, you have bathed, washed

---

[54] Name of dying man

and purified yourself, and dressed in clean and laundered white clothes.

These five symbols need to be seen on the forehead of the figurine as well as on the forehead of the daughter:

Then after sunset, carry the abovementioned figurine out of the city and into a lonely and secret place and there, place it in a hole, which should be really clean and which has been dug in the earth in advance for this purpose and which should be facing towards the East. Then, take a round lead plate, eight to nine inches in diameter on which the five symbols above have been inscribed and place this lead plate on top of the head of the figurine, so that it covers both her and the girl completely.

When you have done this, trace a circle in the earth with the point of a new knife with a white handle, which has been made explicitly for this purpose. This circle must be traced at the distance of one cubit from the abovementioned figurine and you should step into the circle with two faithful companions and perfume around the circle with laudanum and galbanum, after which, you should say the following conjuration.

"*Conjuro te Alma simptea, pura et decora Splendidissima per Deum omnipotem tuum, et ómnium invisibilum Creatorem, et per omnia quæ ipse creavit ab initio mundi, et per Cœlum et Terram et Mare et omnia quæ in eis sunt, et existum, et per has imagines et figuras pro amere tuo et filiæ tuæ fabricatas, quæ ante nos sunt, ut tuam propriam filiam loquentem tecum ad nos addumas, et super plumbi laminam et imaginem eam in forma sponsæ puellæ stare facias, sicut conscievisti, ut nobis det responsum de omnibus rebus, de quibus interrogaverimus eam."*

When you have done this, a Spirit should appear in the form of a very beautiful woman, leading another Spirit with her in the form of a young enchantingly beautiful girl, who along with the first Spirit was covered with the lead plate. Ask what you will and make your wishes clear to her and she should give you a fitting and satisfying response.

After this, you should pray and try to engage the same Spirits so that they can consecrate and validate the abovementioned figurines for you, as well as the lead plate that covers them. Because if you manage to achieve this, then the figurines and the plaque should produce some astonishing results, so that wherever you carry them, you should receive anything you need, merely with a simple summonsand without having to resort to a conjuration. In addition to this, these Spirits will always come to anywhere you are to be found with the aforementioned figurines, day or night and simply by asking and they will always give you a truthful reply. You can gain the goodwill of everyone with these figurines, from men as well as women, by simply touching their flesh and if someone has been arrested, tied and bound, his fetters would fall away simply by touching them. The lead plate alone is so effective, that if anyone were to carry it on his person, he would be guaranteed to never be wounded from any weapon in a war and simply by touching an epileptic, his epilepsy would be cured. And if a person carries the plate to some place where there is hidden treasure, all the enchantments and chains preventing you from digging it up would be destroyed and all the Spirits would be charmed merely by touching it with the plate and so you would easily be able to seize the treasure.

Form of the Circle Above:

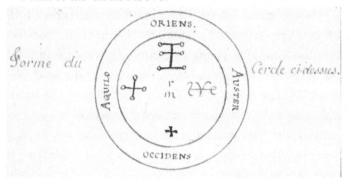

TO RECEIVE A REPLY FROM
A SPIRIT IN A MIRROR

You should take a virgin child, who should be holding a mirror in his right hand and who has been washed, cleaned and dressed, as so should you be too, dressed in extremely clean and perfumed clothes. And when you have made the perfumes for use according to the Art, stroke the forehead of the child in circular movements, hold your hand on top of his head and say these words:

> *"Signo te, puer, in nomine Dei omnipotentis et signet te ipse Deus omnia membra signo fortitudinis et virtutis suæ, sicut signavit electos suos a facienda mirabilia ejus, ita te ipso signet, custodiat, et conservet ab omnia malo, et ab omni periculo. Amen."*

After you have done that, recite this conjuration over the child:

"Conjuro te juvenum virginem per Deum Patrem omnipotentem; conjuro te per Cœlum et Terram, et per omnia quæ in eis sunt; conjuro te per Angelos, Archangelos, Thronos, Dominationes, Principatis. Vertutes, Potentates, Cherubim et Seraphim, et per omnia sanctissima et ineffabilia nomina Dei Creatoris nostri, Tetragrammaton, On, Elion, Adonay, Alpha et Omega, qui est principium et finis; conjuro te per omnia genera linguarum, et per omnia quæ scripta sum in hoc libro et lecta sum a me atque legentur, quod statim suscipias retineas virtutem et potestatem a Creator omnium rerum, et statim, et subito visibiliter videas, et videre in possis in hoc speculo, et tibi benigni, humilis et inansanti in placida humana forma appariam, stem, atque permeneant, absque, ullo tui tremore, formidire, vel pavere, et absque læsione animæ vel corporis tui, vel omnium inconstantium, Spiritus illi omnes, quos in Dei nomine ac virtute invocavero, et circa omnia illa, de quibus a me fuerint interrogati, pure et aperte, et atsque fallacia de interrogates vel quæsitis verum tibi præbeant responsum, per virtutem et potestatem æterni et summi Dei viventi, in cujus virtute hæc omnia jubentus, seu facimus, et in qua nobis fidelibus hæc talla scire fecit. Amen."

These are the names for the conjured Spirits who appear in the mirror; namely:

"Cobia, Caba, Canbtat, Abraca, Abracola, Tuel, Diel, Quul, Astaroth, Castal, Orish, Laufer, Aller, Laufial, Acansarny, Faral, Adeel, Estel, Aysenel, Sathare,Ssanday, Stimel, Bileth, Athanora, Lastul, Letistel, Veycis, Castaon, Fulcinifer, Tronax, Janifeth, Adus."

We really feel that you should know the special characteristics appropriate to each one of these Spirits, so that you can call them up and subsequently prepare your question, as it would be a mistake to call their names all at the same time. So in this example, we would only name or conjure Cobia with the following conjuration:

"Conjuro te, Cobia, per ea que nunc a me dicta sunt, et dicturus sum, et per omnia sanctissima Dei nomina, quæ scripta sum in hoc libro, et per me lecta sum et errant, et in nomine Dei Patrias omnipotentia, omnium que ejus virtutum, dico et præcipio tibi, Cobia, ut cito et statim conjuratur advenieas in hoc speculo, et huic puero virgini famulo Dei pacifice et quiete appareas, sten, et visibilis permaneas, doner ce quamdiu voluero, et ipsi veritatem ostendas de omnibus rebus, de quibus a me interrogator fueris, absque fallacia, sed potius pure, clare at aporte ut recte intelligaris, illa ut ad interrogate verum nobis præbeas responsum. Alioquis amplius in loco ullo non sit tibi sequies, hoc potestatum habeas remanere in terris, sed includi in profundum abyssi, et in lectum damnationis æternæ, ubi tu cum ministeris tuis sempiternaus tuis, et hæc per virtutem Omnipotentis Dei, qui cuncta gubernat, et talem hominibus contulit potestatem, ut vos Spiritus ubique commorantes in ejus nomine et virtute coerescent, adjuro te, et tibi præcipio ut quidquid vobis præcipitur statim venias, et subito admimpleas, sicut pententiæ ultimæ tremendi dici judicii Dei summi te obedire opportebis, et eam inviolabiliter observare."

If he then comes, ask him your question, otherwise you should proceed in the manner that the Art teaches.

To Make The Wonderful
Ring Of Lucibel[55]

On the first day of the waxing of the Moon with an even number[56] with the Sun, go a silversmith's house before sunrise and there you should buy as much cupel silver[57] as you wish in the name of Lucibel and keep it until the fifteenth day when the Full Moon appears.

For the time being, take the silver mentioned and when the Full Moon occurs, make a ring out of it on which you can see the name of Lucibel written. Then go to some deserted place in the mountains, where there is a spring of sweet water coming out of the earth in jets or [boiling] bubbles (you should have searched for this location beforehand). Then take a thread spun by a virgin girl and attach the ring we mentioned to the thread and leave it suspended in the water, at the middle or at the end of a wand of virgin hazelnut until you have finished reciting Psalm 12 *"Usquequo &c"*. But do not say the *"Gloria Patri"*.

When you have done this, take the ring and place it onto a piece of new, white silken cloth, on which you have written these symbols

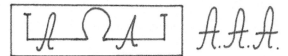

---

[55] Lucibel is an alternative name of Lucifer, found in some of the French witch trials, such as that of Prous Boneta in 1325, and sometimes used by the Cathars.

[56] I.e. the date is an even number like the 2nd, 4th, 6th, etc.

[57] Pure silver extracted from lead based ore.

and after you have perfumed it, wrap the ring in the cloth and keep it in a clean and tidy place that has been perfumed with pleasant scents.

NB. I do not know if you have to write the three "A's" I mentioned on the piece of silk, which are next to the symbols, as they do not seem to have been adapted for this purpose.

1st When you wish to, therefore, make use of the aforementioned ring, put it onto your thumb on your left hand and begin to recite Psalm 12, as mentioned above in a low voice, after which say these words;

"O Lucibel, conjuro te per invisibilem Deum, ut securo modo, et mox debeas me ipsum ferre quo est mea voluntas, scilicet, N.N."

At that moment, you will be transported to the place you have named.

2nd If you then desire to be loved by some person, all you need to do is put on the ring we mentioned above onto your index finger and amongst the words you are going to speak, put in the name of the above person and then, after you have recited the Psalm 12 mentioned above, say,

"O Lucibel, conjuro te per invisibilem Deum et volo ut N.N. me amare facias super omnia mundi."

And at that moment, you will see some results and win her affection.

3rd In a similar way, if you desire to become invisible for anywhere you go, you only need to place the ring mentioned above on the middle finger of your left hand and after you have recited Psalm 12, mentioned above, say:

"O Lucibel, per virtutem hujus annuli tuo nomine confecti volo, ut quousque eum in hoc digito habuero, sim invisibilis quocumque tempore, ac loco, et voluntatem mean possim adimplere."

And at that moment, you will become invisible and you will be able to see others and do everything that you wish without being seen by anyone.

4th In you then wish to play and win at all games, place the ring mentioned above on your ring finger and recite Psalm 12 as above, and say immediately afterwards:

"O Lucibel volo ludere, et quocumque ludo vincere."

And you will see that you will be favoured by Fate.

5th Finally, when you want to receive some revelation about any subject during your sleep, place this ring on your little finger and after you have recited Psalm 12 above, say:

"O Lucibel, hac nocte volo videre et cognoscere N.N...."

... making sure that the room has been cleaned and perfumed.

Whenever you have used this amazing ring, you should always replace it properly in the silken cloth mentioned above and keep it pretty and beautiful.

To Be Invisible

Take a rib from a dead man and with a white handled knife, bought expressly for this purpose, scrape the rib along one side into a point and place these scrapings into fresh ink and with a new pen, write these words on the side:

"Deus Eloy Athanatos, Deus fortis, Deus On, Alpha et Omega, Tetragrammaton, fac me posse transire ut non videas. Amen. Amen. Amen. Fiat. Fiat. Fiat."

Then on the other side, write these symbols:

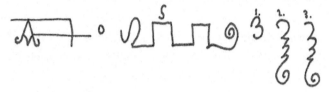

After this, tie the rib to your neck with black silk.

Then take another rib from a dead man, scrape it as you did the first one and place the scrapings into some fresh ink too and with another new feather, write the same symbols on it as on the other, along with your name. Then place a portion of the scrapings on your head. After this, you should grind the rib into a very fine powder, which you will sprinkle on your head as you have done before while keeping the first rib on your person.

AMULET USEFUL AGAINST DIFFERENT
KINDS OF DIFFICULTIES

Take some virgin paper and with the juice of the herb called Celandine, draw the square[58] given on it.

When you have written on this paper in this way, when it is tied to your left shoulder, it will remove any harm caused by evil spells.

You can appear before any Judge with this paper, who will not be able to bring any charges against you or find fault with you.

You will be able to go into battle with complete certainty and you will never be defeated.

It also destroys any evil intention that someone may have against you.

If you place this paper under your head at night, you will see the person who stole anything from you in a dream. You will also see whatever you desire to see.

This ring is also useful for all passions of the soul and body.

In order for this amulet to have all the properties we have just spoken about, you should write on the virgin paper during Thursdays and during the planetary hour of Jupiter. This paper should be tainted black with saffron beforehand and draw the square on it with black lettering, using celandine juice mixed with soot.

Note that when this amulet is used in order to gain knowledge of anything during the night, place it under your head and say this prayer:

---

[58] It seems that the square was not reproduced.

"O Domine Deus per virtutes istius figuræ rogo te ut ostendas mihi (   )."[59]

And you should write the same thing on another piece of paper, which you also place under your head.

EXPERIMENT TO KNOW WHAT THE TIME IS

Take a goblet of clear crystal and then take a wedding ring of a woman who was a virgin when she married, if possible, otherwise take what you can get, provided that it has been blessed. Then suspend this ring by a double white thread in this goblet and hold the thread in both hands with both elbows leaning on the table and gently lower the ring until it is halfway into the goblet and then say these words over the ring in a semi low voice:

"Ecce enim veritatem dilexisti, incerta et occulta sapientiæ tuæ manifesta mihi. What time is it?"

And repeat the same words until you see the ring move by itself and tap out the hours, the half hour and the quarter hour against the inner sides of the goblet.[60]

TO WIN AT GAMES

During a day of Tuesday when the Moon is waxing, buy a piece of lamb meat and give the butcher the price he asks for but make sure that you do not eat it and that while you are

---

[59] Insert name of person saying the prayer.
[60] This is known as dactylomancy, or divination by wedding ring.

paying for it, make sure that you pay with just one coin, whose value should be worth more than the meat. With the change the butcher gives you, make a seal or have one made, on which this character is engraved

on one side and your name written in full on the other and you will see wonders.

The seal may be bigger than this drawing, if you so wish. Also write these words on the piece of virgin paper with wolf's blood: *"Ybac, Abac, judas, Ayda, Aba, Velico terra, Abhac Abac vel Abazar."*

And while holding this paper in your hand, touch the dice or the cards and then all you need to do is ask them for what you wish for in a low voice and what you have asked for will transpire.

FOR GAMES OF CHANCE

Write these names on a piece of virgin paper on a day of Friday and during the waxing of the Moon before sunrise:

"Bun, Baca, Bato, Bati, Produtza, Pro Vicet."

At this point, you can add a conjuration adapted for the subject in question.

TO RECEIVE GOODWILL AND FAVOURS

FROM SOMEONE

On a day of Wednesday at the New Moon, get a virgin child (boy or girl)who knows how to write, to write the *"Pater Noster"* only up to these words, *"Panem nostrum &c"* and then to continue to write Psalm No 3, which begins, *"Deus, in nomine tuo salvum me fac &c."* but without writing the *"Gloria Patri."*

When this has been done, fold the paper up and place it on a newly born child, who is about to be baptised. When he has been baptised, remove it and safeguard it for later use.

When you wish to use it, you only need to touch the person with this paper, man or woman, from whom you have lost good graces (favours) and this person will be forced to condescend to your wish, even if it is in spite of himself.

Note that the solution used to write on the paper we have mentioned above, must be made from rose water mixed with saffron and the feather pen must be ripped from the left wing of a swallow.

IDEM[61]

On a day of Friday, start to write the following prayer on a piece of virgin parchment which you also should recite, on the same day and with great devotion, having first been properly purified in body and soul. Then when you wish to obtain something form someone, take him hand.

---

[61] For the Same.

Here is the prayer:

"Pater On, noster Jehova, qui es Agla in cœlis, Agios Sanctificetur Alpha nomen tuum, Theos adveniat Athanatos regnum tuum, Eleison fiat Imas voluntas tua Caritas sicut in cœlo Panton, et in terra Craton. Panem nostrum Elion quotidianum Homosion da nobis hodic Salvator, et dimitte nobis Redemptor debita nostra Primogenitus sicut et nos Paracletus debitoribus nostris Sabaoth dimittimus Eloym et ne nos Adonay inducas in tentationem Pater, sed libera nos Filius a malo Amen Spiritus Sanctus."

TO RECEIVE AFFECTION FROM
KINGS AND OTHER GREAT PEOPLE

Take some rose oil and recite Psalm No. 4 over it *"Cum invocarem &c"* and rub your face three times with this oil and then go to speak to the Squire or other Lord and you will receive what you wish.

To gain some usefulness or receive some service from someone without any prejudice, say these two words, *"Comisthonon, Sedalay"*, but you should not utter them for any other purpose.

FOR LOVE

Write these names on an apple or a pear or a peach with a new needle, *"Astoroth, Astoroth, Astoroth, impone virtutem tuam huic (   ) per nomen magnum Adonay."*

Then perform a decent conjuration for it and perfume it with wood of Aloes and give it to her to eat, or if you can't make her eat it, show it to her.

IDEM

On a Thursday during the Planetary Hour of Jupiter and while the Moon is waxing, take five drops of blood from the little finger of your left hand and blend it with finely powdered nutmeg. Let this mixture dry in the sun and then when you have ground it to a powder, give it to the person to eat in either a stew or in a drink.

TO BE LOVED EITHER BY A WOMAN

OR BY EVERYONE ELSE.

Take a rib from a man or a woman, according to the person you are performing the ritual for, which can be easily found in a cemetery. Then during a Thursday at the hour of Jupiter, place this rib into running water of a river, or even into a new pot glazed in white, filled with clear and clean water, which has been changed every day in the evening until the evening of the first hour of Saturday night. Then write these names with these symbols on the rib we mentioned above:

"Samuel, Zeel, Fasquali, Hasy, Castiel, Amazel, Camel, Fedicia.

$$C.7.3 \gg .7s$$

Figiel, Zezat,   *Possi susona adferte mihi*
N.N. (name, surname and the mother's name) ad hunc locum."

Then expose the mentioned rib to heat on a fire that you
have lit beforehand, while saying:

> *"I conjure you, you names, which are written on this rib by the*
> *power of He who has created you and who has given you power,*
> *that as this rib with your names on it heats up, so in the same*
> *way will you make N.N. heat up with love for me, so that she*
> *may never have any rest nor peace until she has fulfilled my*
> *wish and has done what I wish of her, which is (   )."*

Make sure that the rib does not burn, as many bad things
will ensue if it does.

And when you have received what you desire, place the
rib into the same pot, whose water you should have changed
beforehand, so that the person's passion may be extinguished
towards you.

To Make A Good Angel Appear,
Who Will Reply To Any
Questions Asked Of Him

Take seven swallows, burn them to a cinder in a new pot that has been haggled for.[62] Grind these charred remains into a very fine powder and make some ink from it using this method:

In a new beaker, mix the powder mentioned above with some garden parsley juice and add some rosewater, so that the ink does not become too thick. Mix all of this well together in the glass and with this tincture write the following symbol on a strip of yellow copper or in its absence, on a strip of red copper called a rosette:

When this symbol has dried, place the strip of metal in a vase filled with pure water and add three laurel seeds into it

---

[62] This is unusual as it goes against the normal approach of never haggling for magical tools.

and place the vase onto a tripod over a new fire, so that it heats up a little. After that place the vase on a table and stir the water with a little rod made of hazel wood and utter these words ten times:

"*Pakalli, aller, yemulet, Wayercigeo, yemileh, Ereindugen gua Kebukim ie dedem.*"

When you have uttered these words ten times, wait a while and you will hear a soft and pleasant voice. When you cry for joy, the good Angel or Spirit will cry for joy with you. Ask him anything that you wish to know and you will have a sure response about all of it.

When you have nothing left to ask him, say to him, "*Go now in the name of God. The Peace of God be with you.*"

After this, pour the water away and when you would like to perform this ritual again, write it out as you did the first time. This is why it is important to safeguard the powder and the ink carefully and when it becomes dry, you can refresh it with rose water and the juice of celery or wild opium poppy

.

Treatise Of
Mixed Cabalah
Which comprises the
Angelic Art
Taken From
Hebrew Sages

Concerning
Miscellaneous Cabalah

This part of the Cabalah consists of Divine Favour by which the Human Spirit, focused on itself while meditating on Celestial matters, finds itself enraptured in a kind of ecstasy, in which it receives revelations of higher sciences and occult matters, which have not been given to the whole of Mankind to know.[63]

Once Mankind has experienced this ecstasy, he can scarcely remember things from the lower world, which equally also contribute to the glory of God and to the benefit of those close to him: the satisfaction, which he experiences seeing himself so close to the Angels takes the place of everyone else.

In order to succeed in being granted such a distinguished favour from Heaven, it would be proper to have some kind of knowledge of the attributes of God, such as the ones the Hebrew Sages have handed down to us. They describe the Divinity as being reconciled in the infinite distance from its centre and as always, is occupied with the reproduction of things.

God being considered as contemplative within himself, cannot only not be described in any manner, but also cannot be understood through Mankind's ability to comprehend. This is why God, when he spoke to Moses, said to him, *"Posterior mea videbis."* Meaning by these words, that Moses cannot know the face of God, seeing that only the eyes of God himself can see it. The Hebrews called it *"Ain Soph"*[64], that is to say, *"the Incomprehensible Infinity"*.

Therefore, the Hebrew Sages wanted to show God as being occupied in the creating things, and he has given ten principle attributions called Numerations, which comprise all things and are like ornaments surrounding him, which make his Divinity shine and which make him known to Mankind.

---

[63] This is an interesting description which could apply to the prophetic state known as Ruach haQadosh (lit. Spirit of Holiness).
[64] Limitless Light, the second of the three Veils of Negativity prior to creation.

These ten Numerations or ornaments [65] have a direct relation with the ten names of God, which precede the ten Angelic Orders, the ten Celestial Spheres and from which the tangible world is consisted, as well as the ten parts of the Microcosm.

The 1st Numeration or ornament of God, which at the same time is the Crown of all the Ages, is called [ ][66], that is to say, Canal, by which God influences and extends his will over the Choir of the Seraphim and over the first Moving Body by means of the Intelligence called Metatron-Serapanim, which means Prince of the Aspects, by means of which, the Hebrews also claimed that God had spoken to Moses. This 1st Numeration relates to the name of God Eihe, which means Essence,[67] because he gives being to all things which exist and fills the entire Universe with the splendour of his Infinite Majesty from the centre to its circumference.

The 2nd Numeration is called Chokmah, that is to say, Wisdom. The name of God appropriate for him is the infallible Name of the four letters Jehovah[68] united at Yod. It is through this that God influences the Cherubim in the star-studded Heaven through the medium of the Angel Raziel, Spirit of Adam, while forming these indefinable lights of the ideal world and consequently distinguishing Chaos from created things.

The 3rd Numeration is called Binah, or Prudence. It relates to the name of God Elohim. By this Numeration, God

---

[65] The 10 Sephiroth of the Tree of Life.

[66] Although blank, this would logically be Kether ("the Crown"), the first Sephira on the Tree of Life, though the Hebrew word for canal is 'teala'.

[67] More frequently translated as "I am".

[68] Yod Heh Vav Heh, the Tetragrammaton.

influences the Choir of the Thrones through the medium of the Angel Zaphkiel, who was the Spirit of Noah, dominating the Sphere of Saturn, where the forms of the first matter were imprinted and from which ensued the birth of the Universe.

The 4th Numeration is called Clemency or Benignancy[69] attributed to the righteous and infinite mercy of God. It bears the name of God El and through it, God influences the Order of the Dominations through the medium of the Angel Zadkiel, who was the Spirit of Abraham and influences the Sphere of Jupiter.

The 5th Numeration is called [ ][70], that is to say, Rigour or Severity. It bears the name of God Gibor and influences the Order of Powers and on the Sphere of Mars through the medium of the Angel of Camael, its Intelligence, who was the Spirit of Samson. It is from this Numeration that the Elements proceed.

The 6th Numeration bears the name of God Eloha, united at Va'Daath.[71] It has an influence over the Orders of Virtues and over the Sphere of the Sun through the medium of the Angel Raphael, its Intelligence, who was the Angel of the Patriarch Isaac and of Toby, his son.

The 7th Numeration is called [ ][72], that is to say, Triumph. It bears the most holy name of the Four Letters,[73] reunited at Sabaoth. It has an influence over the Order of the Principalities and over the Sphere of Venus through the medium of Haniel, its Intelligence and all plants proceed from it.

---

[69] The fourth Sephira is Chesed.

[70] Again, the blank is in the text, but refers to the Sephira Geburah.

[71] An alternative name for Tiphereth.

[72] The text is blank, though the missing Sephira is Netzach.

[73] The Tetragrammaton, giving the divine name Jahveh Sabaoth.

The 8th Numeration bears the name of God Elohim Sabaoth. It has an influence over the Choirs of the Archangels and over the Sphere of Mercury through the medium of the Archangel Michael, its Intelligence and the Angel of Solomon. It is through this Numeration that all animals proceed.

The 9th Numeration is called [],[74] that is to say, Basis or Foundation. It bears the name of God Sadaï [75] and has an influence over the Choirs of Angels and over the Sphere of the Moon through the medium of Gabriel, its Intelligence, who was the Angel of Daniel. It is through this that the Spirits or Angels are allocated to each man.

The 10th and last Numeration is called Kingdom.[76] It bears the name of God Adonai-Melech, which means Lord and King. It has an influence over the Animastic[77] Order, which the Hebrews called Issim or Heroes, Giants, strong and vigorous men and has an influence over the world through the soul of the Messiah or according to the opinion of others, through Metatron, who was the Angel of Moses.

It is this Numeration that bestows the gift of Prophesy to the spirit of men instructed in the Divine Law and in this Science, because Man can succeed in gaining harmony and affinity with the first Numeration through his understanding of the most elevated and spiritual parts; he gains harmony and affinity with the second through his reason and his discourse; through his superior, concupiscent nature or desire for higher things with the third; through his superior, irascible or zealous nature for divine things with the fourth; through his free, arbitrary nature, with the fifth; through his total

---

[74]The text is blank but clearly the missing word is Yesod.

[75] Shadai.

[76] The Sephira of Malkuth, which translates as Kingdom.

[77] Pertaining to mind or spirit; spiritual.

preoccupation with celestial things with the sixth; through the concern he has with inferior things with the seventh; he will succeed in being in agreement with the eighth, if he unites the two qualities from the preceding two Numerations; by means of this, he can rise up from the active to the contemplative and he will reach the ninth; and through the faculty which he has from his first domicile, or ethereal vehicle, he will be in harmony with the tenth.[78]

Here are the objects on which hang all the deliberations of the Cabalists and which acts as a law for them to attain true Wisdom. It is through the knowledge of these things that you will be successful reading this Book of Life and if you pay attention to everything that we have just said, there you will find the seed of the infallible sciences and the seed of the knowledge of things past present and future.

However, as this science contains Divinity as well as the base nature of Mankind, he would not know how to attain it without divine favour and we are going to see how Mankind can nevertheless rise up to there.

Our soul, according to the Platonists, used to exist in a most blissful state and was graced with all knowledge before descending to unify with our bodies in the intelligible world. But finding itself enveloped with bodily material through this union and with their knowledge being so offended by it, they no longer had any idea about the things it used to contemplate in its preceding state. Yet it is not dispossessed of this knowledge: the man who has the ability to acquire them again,

---

[78] This sequence and its attributions seem to suggest a reversal of the usual sequence of the Tree of Life, with the energy sequence being downwards for realisation rather than upwards. In this it could be seen as a predecessor to the work of Charles Stansfield Jones (Frater Achad) in reversing the Tree of Life in the early twentieth century.

may indeed acquire them. By living a sober and frugal life, removing yourself from all excess and from all blemish, carnal knowledge and concentrating on the object you are about to undertake are all means which contribute greatly to make man's spirit focus on itself and to make him suitable for contemplation, as we have mentioned previously, by which the soul gradually rising up with divine grace beyond his material shell, finally finds itself enraptured in a state of soaring ecstasy, called alienation or divine fury, where it can see the discovery of its first glimpses of knowledge once again. From here, he may follow the miraculous results through the gathering of the Angelic Spirits, so that Mankind, in this state, does or says surprising things, which he no longer remembers after the ecstasy has finished and he then no longer wishes to believe that he has done or spoken such things.

After you have studied the knowledge we have set forth above, you may put certain procedures into practice in order to know whatever you desire from the Angels. You have recourse to the miscellaneous Mystery for this, which derives from Cabalah, although it does not depends upon it absolutely and it may be mixed with this kind of Wisdom, which derives from the virtue of superior things and the knowledge of this is called The Divine Law.

In order to put this procedure into practice successfully, you should approach God and his Angels, as we have stated before, through leading a shrewd life and through prayer and you should know all their names.[79]

If you want to have a revelation about some good thing you desire, for example, you should know that there are only certain days when you will be able to perform your rituals and that during each of these days, there is one Angel who

---

[79] I.e. God's and his Angels'.

governs it and one name of God appointed to it and that you should use his name him in your prayer, according to the day you are in and you should do it in the manner given as follows:

The Order Of The Days During Which You Should Work With This Example & The Names Of God Appointed To Them

Wednesday	(Mercury)	Elohim Sabaoth
Saturday	(Saturn)	Elohim
Tuesday	(Mars)	Elohim Gibor
Friday	(Venus)	Sabaoth Jehovah
Monday	(Moon)	Sadaï[80]
Thursday	(Jupiter)	El
Sunday	(Sun)	Eloa Va-daath

Names Of The Angels Appointed To The Days Mentioned Above

Wednesday.. Raphael

Saturday... Cassiel

Tuesday... Samael

Friday... Anael

Monday... Gabriel

Thursday...Sachiel

Sunday...Michael

---

[80] Shadai

Being prepared in this manner with a clean heart and without having sinned, as we have mentioned above, you should perform the ritual for eight days in the order of the days indicated above, which should be chosen only during the waxing of the Moon. Leave an interval of two days between one ritual and the next and if you cannot complete everything during one single Lunar month, you should finish it during the next waxing of the Moon.

You should therefore begin on a Wednesday, which should be a clear and serene day, during which you should fast on bread and water, your room should be very clean and you should be washed. You should rise one hour before Sunrise and while dawn breaks, you should recite the following prayers on your knees, seven times each day so that they are finished before Sunrise. During these prayers, you should change the name of God and the Angel appointed to the day you are working in.

On the following Saturday, which should be the second day for performing your ritual, you should rise at the same time as before and say the same prayers as before, in which you will previously have taken care to insert the name of God and Angel appointed to that day. And you should follow the same method for all the other days until the end.

You will therefore perform the 1st Invocation to God.

To raise up our hearts to God and to draw his condescendence upon us.

Psalm 8[81]

Domine Dominum noster, quam admirabile est nomen tuum in universa terra, quæ dedit confessionem tuam super cœlos.

---

[81] This version of Psalm 8 has a number of differences from the traditional version.

Ex ore infantium et lactantium finiasti virtutem propter inimicos tuos, ut deteres inimicum et ultorem.

Quoniam videbo cœlos tuos oper digitorum tuorum, Lunam et Stellas quæ tu fundasti.

Quid est homo quod memor es ejus? Aut filius hominis quoniam visitas eum?

minuisti eum paulominus ab Angelis gloria et decore coronasti eum.

Et constituisti cum Dominatorum in operibus manuum tuarum. Omnia subiecisti sub pedibus ejus, oves et boves universas insuper et quadrupdes campi.

Volucres cœli et pisces maris qui pertransenntes semitas maris.

Domine Dominus noster, quam admirabile est nomen tuum in universa terra.

Prayer to God
Psalm 103[82]

Benedic, anima mea, Domino (here you insert the name of God allocated to the day) Domine Deus meus magnificatus es vehementer, confessionem et decorem induisti. Induens lumine sicut vestimentum, extendens cœlos sicut cortinam.

Qui tegis in aquis superiora ejus; qui ponis nubes cursum, tuum qui ambulas super pennas venti.

Qui facis Angelos tuos spiritus, Ministros tuos ignem urentem.

Fundasti terram super bases ejus, non commovebitur in æternum et semper.

Abysso velut vestimento operuisti eam; super montes stabunt aquæ.

Ab increpatione tua fugient, a voce tonitrui tui præcipitabuntur.

---

[82] Again this version of Psalm 103 has a number of textual differences. The numbering is based on the Greek Septuagint Psalms, so it is 104 in the Masoretic Hebrew Psalm numeration.

Ascendent montes, descendent valles ad locum quem fundasti eis.

Terminum posuisti, quem non transgredientur, neque revertentur ut operiant terram.

Qui emittis fontes in convallibus, inter montes ambulabunt.

Potabunt omnes bestiæ agri, et extinguent onagri sitim suam.

Juxta illos volucres cœli habitabum de medio frondium dabunt vocem.

Irrigans montes de excelsis suis de fructu operum tuorum satiabitur terra.

Faciens germinare jumentis et herbam servituti hominum.

Ut educant panem de terra, et vinum lætificet cor hominis.

Ut illustrem faciem in oleo, et panis cor hominis confirmet .

Saturabuntur ligna campi, Cedri Libani quas plantavit.

Quoniam ibi passeres nidificabunt, Ciconiæ abietes domus ejus.

Montes excelsi Cervis, petra refugium Cuniculis.

Fecisti Lunam propter tempora, Sol cognovit occasum suum.

Posuisti tenebras et facta est nox, in ipsa movebuntur omnes bestiæ saltus.

Catuli leonum rugient ad prædam, et ut quærant a Deo escam suam.

Orientur Sol et congregabuntur, et in habitaculis suis accumbent.

Egredietur homo ad opus suum, et ad culturam suam usque ad vesperam.

Quam multiplinta sum opera tua, Domine, omnia illa in sapientia fecisti, impleta est terra possession tua.

Huc mare magnum et spatiosum minibus; illic reptilian, quorum non est numerous, et animalia pusilla cum magnio.

Illi naves pertransibum, Leviathan quem formasti ut videat in ipso.

Omnia illa te expectant, ut descibum eis in tempore suo .

Dabia illis, colligent, aperies manum tuam, saticbuntus bons

Avertenie autem te faciem tuam turbabuntus, auferes spiritum
corum peribunt, et in pulverem suum revertentur.

Emittes spiritum tuum in me (here the name of the person who
is praying must be named) et creabur, et renovabis faciem meam.

Sit Gloria Domini in æternum, lætetur Dominus in operibur
suis.

Qui respicit terram, et contremiscet, tanget monter et
fumigabunt.

Cantabo Domino in vita mea psalllam Deo meo quamdiu fuero.

Inundum sit ei eloquium meum, ego vero lætabor in Domino.

Deficiant peccatores e terra, et impii amplius non sint: Benedic
anima mea, Domino. Alleluia.

Prayer

Omnipotem æterne Deum, qui totam Creationam condidisti in
laudem tuam, et honorem tuum, ac ministerium hominis, oro te
atque obrero, ut Spiritum (here insert the name of the Angel of
the day) emitter digneris, qui me doceal quæ illum cum justitia
et pretate interrogavero. Verum non mea fiat voluntar, sed tua
per nomen sanctissimum tuum, quod exaltetur per omnia
sæcula.

Prayer to the Angel

O bone Angele (you name the Angel of the day here) qui es
præpositur Diei (you name the day you are in here) te deprecor,
ut Dominum Deum tuum et meum, qui in te potentiam et
fortitudinem super omnibus ingenium et vigorem posuit,
supplicer, ut concedere mihi dignetur hunc artem Kabala (or
another science) et quod mihi assistas in meo auxilio, et accipias
meum hoc nomen (that is to say, the name of the person who is
praying) quod confirmo super te, ut perficias omne mecum velle,
et illumine et doceas quæ operaturus ero in hac scientia. Amen.
Amen. Amen. Fiat. Fiat.Fiat.

CONCERNING
MISCELLANEOUS CABALAH

2ND PART

In this second part, we are concerned with how to deal with the Seals, Pentacles or Heptacles, which you must wear hung around your neck, so that you can obtain the graces you are seeking.

In order to create them in such a way that you are guaranteed success, you should be fully prepared, as we have said in the 1st Part and you should abstain from all sin during 7 lunar months, this number being mystical and of great value and power in the Cabalistic Rituals. You should take care not to use these things, except in case of great necessity and to avoid performing these experiments merely out of curiosity. Because it will be to the detriment of the person carrying them out. For it is written: *Non accipies nomen Domini Dei tui in vanum.*

CONCERNING THE MATERIALS
SUITABLE FOR THESE RITUALS

There are three different kinds of materials, which you can use in order to create the Heptacles, which is what we are dealing with here: namely, pure gold, purer silver and virgin wax, on which you need to engrave verses form Scripture, appropriate for the result you are aiming to achieve, along with the Names of God and the Names of the Angels necessary to get results, as we will discuss later on. And whoever creates these Heptacles with a pure heart and with the method that we are going to mention, will be astonished by their effectiveness, which is greatly superior than other rituals of this genre.

For all illnesses and infirmities of the body, you should use the purest and cleanest virgin wax. As for all other results, you can make use of Gold or Silver; but if you wish to obtain a favour from any Prince, you should use Gold rather than any of the others.

RITUAL

You begin by setting out the thing you wish to obtain, such as goodwill, friendship, honour, wealth, health, victory over your enemies, knowledge, divination, revelation and such like things. Chose one of the three materials listed above and although it is better to begin on a Saturday, the Pentacle will have a better effect, however, if you begin the ritual on the day of the governing Planet, which directly influences the object in question, as in the example below.

Having chosen an appropriate and corresponding day, you should have everything ready before sunrise, including a newly lit fire, so that you can purify the material and before lighting the fire, you should bless the material while reciting the following prayer below, seven times.

BLESSING PRAYER[83]

"Domine quam multiplicati sum tribulantes me, multi insurgents adversum me.

Multi dicunt animæ meæ, non est salua ipsi in Deo solo.

Tu antem, Domine, susceptor es pro me, gloria mea, et exaltrans caput meum.

Voce mea ad Dominum clamabo, si respondet mihi de monte sanctitatis ejus.

Ego jacui et dormivi, exsurrexi quoniam Dominus sustentabit me.

Non timebo prælia populorum, qui in circuita positi sumt adversium me.

Exurge, Domine, salvum me fac Deus meus, quoniam percussisti omnes inimicos meos in maxilta, dentes impiorum confregisti.

Domini est salus super hanc creaturam (here you name the material) benedicto tua solo.

Ecce nunc benedicte Dominum omnes servi Domini ; qui statis in domo Domini in noctibus extolite manus vestras ad sanctitatem et benedicte Dominum.

Benedictat te creatura (here, insert the name of the material) Dominus ex Sion, qui fecit cœlum et terram.

---

[83] This prayer is composed of Psalm 3 verses 2-9 followed by an adaption of Psalm 134(133).

Hæc creatura (here, you name the material again) accipiet
benedictionem a Domino, et misericordiam a Deo salutari suo.
Etenium benedictionem dabit legislator, ibunt de virtute in
virtutem (you name the material here) videbitus Deus Deorum
Sion.
Quoniam illic mandavit Dominus benedictionem et vitam
usque in sæculum."

Oremus
"Sapientia tua, Domine Deus cuncta disposita atque omnia tua
virtute et gratia perficiantur, creaturam istam (here you insert
the name of the material) benedic, Domine, et sanctifica, ut in
conspectu tuo quidquid eis peragimus ad omnium inimicorum
tuorum incursus exsurgamus victores, per nomen
Sanctissimum tuum quod exaltum sit in sæcula. Amen."

After you have recited this benediction seven times over
the material, as we have mentioned above, while covering the
material with your right hand but without touching it,
however, you should throw it onto the fire in a new pot of
either earth or iron. And as soon as it is on the fire, perform
some sweet-smelling fumigations over it, if your purpose is
for obtaining good things, or really stinking fumigations, if
your purpose is for evil things. As soon as you have done the
fumigation and while the material is melting over the fire, you
should recite the two Prayers, which have been written[84]
above taking care the change the Names of God and Angels in
them, appropriate to the day and for the objective, which you
are trying to achieve.

---

[84] The original text has the words "on page 17" here, which we have
removed as we do not have the same pagination.

Take note, that during the fumigations (which must also be done seven times each day), you should pronounce the Scriptural Verses appropriate to the objective for which you are working with each of the fumigations, such as those you will see later on.

When that has been done and as soon as you see that the wax has melted, or that the metals are really red, you should throw them into white wine bought expressly for this purpose, which is called for the purification of the material. This purification is repeated for each of the mornings, seven times in the same way and with the same prayers, in which you only change the names of the day, as we have pointed out to you beforehand and all of this is repeated for seven consecutive days. But on the last day, instead of using white wine to purify the material, you should use blessed water.

Note again, that the instant you throw the material into the white wine or into the rose water, you should also recite the same scriptural verses you recited during the fumigations.

This ritual is always performed while turned towards the East.[85]

When you have blessed and purified the material in this way with much devotion and with a strong intention to implant the quality you desire into it, you should wait until the eighth day, during which, always before sunrise, you should light the fire and bless is while saying:

"Benedic, Domine, hanc creaturam ignis, ut valeat ad effectum quem peto a Benitate tua, atque omnipotentia tua per nomen Sanctissimum tuum quod exaltatur per omnia sæcula. Amen."

---

[85] Literally the direction of the Rising Sun.

Immediately place the material onto the fire or into the fire and you should suffumigate seven times, repeating the verses from the Holy Scriptures appropriate to the subject seven times. And while the material is melting, you should recite the prayer to God and to the Angels of the Day,[86] and when you see that it has melted, you should throw it into the mould, which has been prepared in advance for this purpose. And at the same time, you should recite the verses of the Scripture again, adding the following words:

> "*Omnipotens æterne Deus, esto propitious mihi N.N. famulo tuo, et vos omnes Angeli Dei, quorum nomina inscripta manem in hoc signaculo (here you insert the name of the material) istote mihi in auxilium ad obtiendum (you name here what you wish to obtain) per Sanctissima Nomina et per omnes virtutis Domini Dei Creatoris nostril, qui exaltetur in sæcula.*"

If the material you are using for the Pentacle is wax, mix some appropriate ingredients to treat the sickness you wish to heal into it while it is in a melted state, as for example, when you are treating sores or ulcers, mix rose oil into it and other things suitable for them and you should do the same for other sicknesses. Apply this wax over the sick part, which should be healed after seven days without fail.

You must especially note the most valuable benefit that exists in using wax Pentacles. This is because they can also be useful for a third person[87] who may be some distance away, provided that you mention his situation in your prayers. In order to produce this result, you should bring some of the

---

[86] Again, the original text has the words "page 17" here.

[87] This is an interesting early example of absent healing.

absent sick person's blood, hold the Pentacle above it and recite the following words to it:

> *"Esto nobis Domine Pater Liberator noster in omnibus infirmitatibus nostris propter ineffabilem misericordiam tuam, et vos Angeli Dei potentes virtute qui facitis voluntatem ejus, et quorum nomina inscripta manem in hoc Signaculo, adiuro vos ut per omnia quæ ipse creavit, et ider per virtutem vestram auxilium statim adferatis (here, you name the sick person) ut salvus et liberaveat ab infermitate sua (here, you name the sickness and the sick part, if the sickness inhabits a particular part of the body) qua corpus suum nunc laberat, et ab omni malo. Amen. Amen. Amen."*

Then finish by reciting the appropriate verses of Scripture for the illness which should also be written on the Pentacle.

This method for healing sicknesses works sympathetically, and you can find these things explained in the books about the secrets of Nature and in the books about Physicians. And although this method appears impossible to those who do not know how to fathom the secrets of the mixed mysteries, we must however believe that it is done in this way because the rituals (which teach us to understand how to remedy or alter the state of a distant subject on which we are working) have a direct correspondence and a tendency to produce the same effect, especially if they are done with intention, so that they can act upon the distant subject with even more power than the intent and power of the person performing the ritual, as a part of the same power is found in the hands of the person performing the ritual and he retains a portion of the subtle spirits of the sick individual and the appropriate words he uses have an effect on his state of health and this is how the result is imparted. These words by themselves would remain inanimate, instead when they are pronounced over the body or over part of the body, they become animate and effective and can produce either good or ill, depending on what you wish to achieve.

CONCERNING THE METHOD FOR MAKING THE

PENTACLE OR HEPTACLE[88]

We call this Pentacle a *"Heptacle"*, because it is composed of seven angles, as you can see in the figure below.

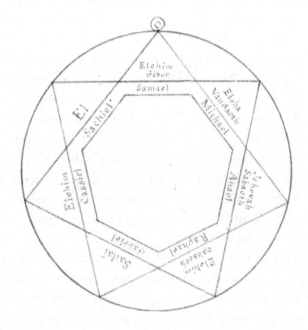

NB: You could also write all the names in Hebrew, which would be better, as this is the language preferred by Spirits.

---

[88] It is actually a heptagon inside a heptagram.

In the first angle around the circumference, you write the names of God, beginning with Elohim Gibor and then followed by the others. Then within the others, you write the names of the seven Angels of God and lastly in the centre you write the verses from Scripture appropriate to the matter being requested, such as you will find described later on.

We have said above that you can begin the ritual on a Saturday and finish it on the following Saturday, which as you know, is the last day after the Creation, when the Creator was pleased with his works. But if you wish to make much more powerful Pentacles, you should begin on the day of a Planet whose influence is favourable to your planned objective. For example, supposing that you wish to create a Pentacle with the intention appropriate for obtaining the favour of some Prince, then you should begin during the day of Sunday, before sunrise and you should continue the ritual for seven days and on the eighth day, which should be the following Sunday, you will create the Pentacle in the manner which we have described, while continually making sure to place the Name of God and the name of the Angel of the day in the first space at the top of the Pentacle. As in this example, you should place the name of Eloha Va-daath at the top for the day of Sunday and the name of Michael, which corresponds to that day.

Similarly, if you wish to be victorious against your adversaries, enemies or in legal cases, you should place the name of Elohim Gibor at the top and below you should place the name of Samael, who is the Angel of Mars and in this case, you should begin your ritual on a Tuesday.

From all that we have just mentioned, you can see that because this second Section of *Miscellaneous Cabalah* can be a bit complicated, it is really important to study it well, so that you do not make any mistake when putting it into practice. And so you can be even more confident, it would be very useful and very handy to make yourself some kind of set formula for each day, so that you can adapt the prayers for them and from your experiments, you should be able to see that you will be well compensated for your pains which you will have given yourself through the marvellous results you are going to obtain.

Finally and lastly, you must note that the results we are aiming for, before you start working with distant healing, is obtained through staring at the person and by touching his body, if at all possible, as well as other similar things.

PROPERTIES OF THE VERSES & SCRIPTURE[89]

1. In order to be well received by Princes, Lords and others
    Narrabo statutum, Dominus dixit ad me: Filius meus es tu, ego hodie genui te.
    Postula a me et dabo gentes hæreditatem tuam, et possessionem tuam terminos terræ.[90]

2. In order to be warmly welcomed by all men
    Exultabimus, Domine, in virtute tua, cantabimus et psallemus potentiam tuam.[91]

3. In order to be raised up with Dignity by everyone
    Dominus custodiet eum et vivicabit eum: beatus fiet in terra, et non trades eum in animam inimicorum ejus.[92]

---

[89] As with elsewhere, the wording of the Psalms may vary slightly from traditional versions, and for this reason we have included the Psalm numbers for ease of reference.
[90] Psalm 2:7-8.
[91] Psalm 21(20):14.

1. In order to be pleasing to all men and to obtain their favours
    Quoniam Dominus excelsus, terribilis, Rex magnus super omnem terram.
    Comprimet populos sub nobis et Regna sub pedibus nostris.[93]

4. In order to gain the affection of Princes, Lords and of all men and to be pleasing to them
    Florebit in diebus suis Justus, et multitude pacis donet non sit Luna.
    Et dominabitur a mari usque ad mare, at a flumine usque ad terminos terræ.[94]

5. In order to be named for Dignities of this World
    Exaltabitur sine unicornis cornu meum, conspersursum oleo viridi.
    Justus ut palma florebit, sicut Cedrus Libani multiplicabitur.[95]

6. So that no person may refuse you an honest question
    Et ego semper tecum, tenuisti manum dexteram meam. Tu consilium tuum deduces me, et postea in Gloria assumes me.[96]

7. To resist domestic enemies
    Ego jacui et dormivi, exsurrexi quoniam Dominus sustentabit me.
    Non timebo prælia populorum qui in circuitu positi sum adversum me.[97]

---

[92] Psalm 41(40):3.
[93] Psalm 47(46):3-4.
[94] Psalm 72(71):7-8.
[95] Psalm 92(91):11, 13.
[96] Psalm 73(72):23-24.
[97] Psalm 3:6-7.

8. To throw lying or treacherous men off your scent

Quoniam non Deus volens iniquitatem tu es, non habitabit juxta te malignus.

Perdes loquentes mendacium, virum sanguini et frandir abominabitur Dominus. [98]

9. In order to recover hidden objects

Immensæ sunt gentes in fovea quam fecerum, in rete quam absconderunt captus est peseorum.

Notum Dominus fecit judicium: in opere palmarum suarum illaqueatus est impius. Sela.[99]

10. To prosper in all things

Dominus sors partir meæ, et calieis mei, tu sustentabis sortem meam.

Funes ceciderunt mihi in jucundia, insuper hæreditas præclara mihi.[100]

11. To be delivered from all trials and tribulations

Ne elongeris a me, quoniam tribulatio proxima, quoniam non est qui me adjuvet.

Tu autem Domine, ne elongeris fortitudo mea in auailium meum festina.[101]

12. To know whether a sick person will die or live

Exultabimus, Domine, in salute tua, et in nomine Dei nostri crigens vexillum impleat Dominus omnes petitiones tuas.[102]

---

[98] Psalm 5:5-7.
[99] Psalm 9:15-16.
[100] Psalm 16(15):5-6.
[101] Psalm 22(21):12, 20.
[102] Psalm 20(19):6-7.

NB. If he is to survive, you will receive your reply within the day; if not, he will die.

13. To be secure while passing through dubious and dangerous places

    Dominus pastor meus animan meam restituet, diriges me per semitas justiciæ propter nomen suum.

    Etiam cum ambulavero per vallem tenebrosam non timebo malum, quoniam tu mecum es, virga tua et pedem tuum ipsa me consolabuntus.[103]

14. To be provided with Food and Lodgings

    Domine, ordinabis in conspetu meo mensam, adversus tribulantes me impinguasti in oleo caput meum, calix meus superabundans.

    Veruntamen bonitas et misericordia sequentur me omnibus diebus vitæ meæ, et quiescam in domo Domini in longitudine dierum.[104]

15. To make a sick man rest

    Anima ejus in bono dormiet, et semen ejus hæreditabit terram.

    Oculi mei semper ad Dominum, quoniam ipse educiet ex rete pedes meos.[105]

16. To prevent being bitten by any dog or serpent

    Me silis sicut equus et mulus, in quibus non est intellectur.

    In chamo et fræno maxillam ejus ut constringas ne appropiunquet ad te.[106]

---

[103] Psalm 23(22):3-4.
[104] Psalm 23(22):5-6.
[105] Psalm 25(24):13, 15.
[106] Psalm 32(31):9.

17. Against persecution from powerful men and from Tyrants

Fiat sicut puivis ante faciem venti, et Angelus Domini expellens.

Sit via illorum tenebræ et lubricum, et Angelus Domini persequens eos.[107]

18. To make a woman yearning for a child give birth without pain

Quam prætiosa misericordia Deus, et filii Adam in umbra alurum tuarum confident.

Quoniam tecum fons vitæ, in lumine tuo videbitur lumen.[108]

19. To confound an enemy who would come against you armed and not harm you

Salus autem justorum a Domino, fortitudo eorum in tempore tribulationis.

Et adjuvabit illos Dominus, et eripiet illos: eripiet illos ab impiis, et salvabit eos, quia speraverunt in eo.[109]

20. To be lucky in all your affairs

Quoniam Dominus excelsus terribilis Rex magnus super omnem terram.

Seliget nobis hæreditatem nostram, magnificentiam Jacob quem dilexit.[110]

21. To protect yourself from wicked judges who persecute the poor iniquitously

---

[107] Psalm 35(34):5-6.
[108] Psalm 36(35):8, 10.
[109] Psalm 37(36):39-40.
[110] Psalm 47(46):3, 5.

Lætabitur Justus, quoniam vidit ultionem; plantas suas lavabit in sanguine impii, et dicet nemo ulique est fructus justo, utique est Deus judex in terra.[111]

22. To obtain things necessary for living
   Nolite sperare in calumnia et rapina; nolite fieri vandas; divitiæ cum affluent nolite cor adponere.
   Et est tibi Domine misericordia, quoniam tu reddes viro secumdum opera ejus.[112]

23. For a man to be rewarded with good things in his family
   Me benedicam te, Dominum, in vita mea, in nomine tuo extollam palmas meas.
   Sicut adipe et pinguedine satiabitur anima mea, et cum labiis exultationis laudabit os meum.[113]

24. To acquire the fruits of the Earth in abundance
   Coronasti annum bonitatis tuæ, et vestigial tua stillabum pinguendinem.
   Vestiem planities pecora, et valles operientur frumento, jubilabunt atque canent.[114]

25. To make it rain at the appropriate time
   Visitasti terram, et irrigasti eam, plurimum dotasti eam; rivulus Dei repletur est aquis: præparabis frumentum eorum, quoniam sic præparabis eam.
   Sulcos ejus inebria, æqua cumulos ejus imbribus lubricam eam redde, germini ejus benedices.[115]

---

[111] Psalm 58(57):11-12.
[112] Psalm 62(61):11, 13.
[113] Psalm 63(62):5-6.
[114] Psalm 65(64):12-13.
[115] Psalm 65(64):10-11.

26. To praise God for the goods of the Earth, which He has granted us and thereby obtain these goods more abundantly for the future

Omnia terra adoret te, et psallat tibi, psallat nomini tuo. Sela
Venite et videte opera Dei terribilis, opera super filios Adam.[116]

27. To give thanks to God for the abundance of the fruits of the Earth

Terra dedit germen suum, benedicat nos Deus Deus noster.
Celebrabunt te propati Deus, celebrabunt te populi omnes.[117]

28. Against dangers of the waters and of the Sea; and to be saved quickly from them

Dixit Dominus ex Basan convertam, convertam de profundis maris.[118]

29. To be lucky in all things

Veritas de terra germinabit, et justitia de cœlo prospexit.
Etiam Dominus dabit bonum et terra nostra dabit fructum suum.[119]

30. To have God as your guardian

Habitans in abdito Altissimi, in umbra omnipotentis commorabitur.
Dicam Domino spes mea et munimentum meum, Deus meus confidam in eo.[120]

---

[116] Psalm 66(65):4-5.
[117] Psalm 67(66):7-8.
[118] Psalm 68(67):23.
[119] Psalm 85(84):12-13.
[120] Psalm 91(90):1-2.

31. Against weapons

Quoniam ipse liberabit me de laqueo venantium, a peste pravitatum.

Ala sua operiet me, et sub pennis ejus confidam sentum et parma veritas ejus.[121]

32. To be safe during all journeys

Quoniam Angelos suos præcipiet adesse mihi, ut custodian me in omnibus viis meis.

Super palmas portabunt me, ne forte offendam in lapidem person meum.[122]

33. To be protected from all beasts and serpents

Super Leonem et Aspidem iter facies, conculiabis catulum Leonis et Draconem.

Quoniam me concupivit eripiam eum, protegam eum quoniam coquovit nomen meum.[123]

34. To conserve goods and honours in your life

Invocabit me respondebo illi, cum ipso sum in tribulation eripiam eum, et glorificabo eum.

Longatudine dierum satiabo eum et ostendam illi salutare meum.[124]

35. To receive God's Wisdom

Notis fecit vias suas Moysi, filiis Israel studia ejus.

Pius et premus gratia, Dominus bentus ira, et magnus misericordia.[125]

---

[121] Psalm 91(90):3-5.
[122] Psalm 91(90):11-12.
[123] Psalm 91(90):13-14.
[124] Psalm 91(90):15-16.
[125] Psalm 103(102):7-8.

36. To rise up out of poverty and to be raised up in honours and riches

Elevans de pulvere inopem, de sircoribus exultabis mendicum.

It collocet eum cum Principibus, cum Principibus populi sui.[126]

37. To go before judgment with firmness against false accusations

You should wash your face and hands before sunrise, then suffumigate all your clothes with sweet-smelling scents and then you may go before the Judges with your trust in God and you should strive to always keep the following verses in your heart and in your mouth as you go:

Domine judica causam animæ meæ et libera vitam meam.

Respice Domine, quantam injustitiam mihi imponit, et adjuva meum jus.[127]

And you will see how the Lord answers the prayers of those who trust in him.

38. To save yourself from pirates and assassins

Quoniam ecce impii intendent arcum, præparaverum sagillas eorum super nervum, ut sagillent rectos corde.

Quoniam Justus Dominus justitias diligit, rectum auspiciet vultus ejus.[128]

39. For the same objective

Respice, responde mihi Dominus Deus meus, illumina seules meos ne quando obdormiam in morte.

Ne quando dicat inimicus meus, prævalui adversus cum tributantes me exultabunt, cum lapsus fuero.[129]

---

[126] Psalm 113(112):7-8.
[127] Psalm 69(68):19.
[128] Psalm 11(10):3, 8.
[129] Psalm 13(12):4-5.

40. Against Highway robbers

Dominus super mea et propugnacutum meum, et cripins me, seutum meum, et cornu salutis meæ proleilio mea.

Laudans invocabo Dominum, et ab inimicis meis salvus ero.[130]

41. To deliver yourself from the midst of your enemies (you should also pronounce these verses)

Ego autem in innocentia mea ambulabo, redime me et miserere me.

Pes meus stetit in rectitudine, in excelsis benedicam Domino.[131]

42. To discover a hidden object

You should take a ring that has neither a bezel nor a stone on it and you should tie it to a piece of thread, which you should suspend in the middle of a glass of water and you should say:

Ecce veritatem direxisti in intentionibus, et in occultis sapientiam notam mihi facias.[132]

43. To prevent serpents from moving

Exsurgat Deus et dissipentur inimici ejus.

When you wish to make it go, say:

Et fugiant qui oderum eum a facie ejus.[133]

44. To win a law suit

Deus adstat in congregatione judicis in medico Deorum judicabit.

Usquequo judicabitis iniquitatem, et facies impiorum suscipietis.[134]

---

[130] Psalm 18(17):3-4.
[131] Psalm 26(25):11-12.
[132] Psalm 51(50):8.
[133] Psalm 68(67):2 (both phrases).
[134] Psalm 82(81):1-2.

VERSES FOR ILLNESSES AND INFIRMITIES

1. **Against Nose Bleeds and Haemorrhages in all other parts of the body**

   Libera me de sanguinibus Deus, Deus salutia meæ, cantabit lingua mea justitiam tuam.[135]

2. **To deliver a sick man from all infirmity**

   Præ vastitatem pauperum præ gemitu menduorum, exiorgam dicit Dominus ponam in salute loquetur pro de ipso.[136]

3. **For the same objective**

   Quoniam circumdederunt Dolores mortis, et congregationes Beliam perterruerunt me.

   Dolorea infermi invenerunt me, prævenerunt offendiculo mortis.

   Et dedisti mihi oculum salutis tua, et dextera tua confortasti me, et mansuetudine tua multiplicasti me.[137]

4. **Against a malevolent fever**

   Domine Deus meus clamavi ad te, et sanasti me.

   Domine exaltasti ex infermo animam meam, vivificasti me, ne descenderem in puteum.[138]

5. **For toothache and bone fractures**

   Quis est vir qui vult vitam, diligit dies et videat bonum?

   Custodit omnia ossa ejus, unum ex his non est fractium.[139]

---

[135] Psalm 51(50):16.
[136] Psalm 12(11):6.
[137] Psalm 18(17):5-6, 36.
[138] Psalm 30(29):3-4.
[139] Psalm 34(33):13, 21.

6. **For blindness**
Cor meum circuivit, dereliquit me virtur mea et lumen oculorum meorum insuper etiam ipsi non sunt mecum.[140]

7. **For muteness**
Non est sanitas in carne mea a facie iræ tuæ, non est pax in ossibus meis a facie peccati mei.
Quoniam iniquitales meæ supergressæ sunt caput meum, sicut onus grave ponderosiores factæ sunt super me.[141]

8. **Against fever**
Dominus confortabit eum super stratum doloris, universum cubile ejus convertisti in infirmitate ejus.
Ego dixi : Domine miserere mei, sana animam meam, quamvis peccaverim tibi.[142]

9. **Against all haemorrhages**
Libera me de sanguinibus, Deus Deus salutis meæ.[143]

10. **Against womens' haemorrhages**[144]
In Deo laudabo verbum ejus in deo speravi, non timebo quid faciat caro mihi.[145]

11. **For headaches**
Quoniam Gloria virtutis eorum tu, et in voluntate tua exaltabis corum nostrum.[146]

---

[140] Psalm 38(37):11.
[141] Psalm 38(37):4-5.
[142] Psalm 41(40):4-5.
[143] Psalm 51(50):16.
[144] Presumably refers to the menses.
[145] Psalm 56(55):5.
[146] Psalm 89(88):18.

12. Against Malaria

Memento mei Domine in bona voluntate erga populum tuum, visita me in salute mea.[147]

13. For a continual fever

Misit verbum suum, et sanavit eos, et liberavit a oruptionibus eos.

Manifestent Dominus misericordiam ejus, et mirabilia ejus filii hominum.[148]

14. To heal all wounds or sores in a short time

Domine omnia a te veiunt tua gatia, quoniam nos sanat, neque germen, neque ceratum, sed verbum tuum est illud justum, et illud quod sanat omniem rem.[149]

---

[147] Psalm 106(105):4.

[148] Psalm 4:2-3.

[149] This does not match any Psalm, the nearest comparison is Psalm 106(105):19-20.

CONCERNING
MISCELLANEOUS CABALAH

3RD PART

This Third Part, which contains Angelic Signs, reveals enough to us through its name alone how important it is to lead a pure and healthy life before beginning with it. And you should always believe yourself to be in the company of the Angels of God and to behave accordingly, as is proper for us to do so when they are with us, just as if they are actually before us and visible to our eyes.

On the day when you want to perform this ritual, you should strive to be free from all sin, even from the forgivable sins, your spirit being completely focused on what you are going to be doing and you should be infused with true belief and humility, while repeating the following from sunrise to sunset often:

"Omnipotens æterne Deus, Fons misericordiæ, propitur esto mihi famulo tuo quam creare dignatur es."

You should take care to fast during that day and only to eat at the permitted hour during these fast days.

When night of that day has fallen, he[150] will enter alone into his chamber, which must be kept very clean, and into which, no person may enter during that day. As he enters into his chamber, he should have a censer in his hand, onto which he will have placed some white incense, some mastic, some wood of aloes and others scents and he should cense the whole room and the other rooms of his dwelling, if he still has any left. Then he will enter back into his chamber, always censing the whole time. As soon as he has performed his censing, he should completely undress and kneel before an image of God with a blessed candle in his right hand and he should recite the following prayer with great devotion and humility:

Prayer to God

"Domine Deus Rex Cœli et Terræ, et Universi Creator, qui solo verbo omnia creasti et hominem ex limo terræ ad imaginem et similitudinum tuum formasti, et Angelos tibi Administratens registi, ut ustriant cum in omnibus viis tuis, ut noms politer ambunt in lege Dei sui, nec prævaruet in mandatis tuis. Tu es ille Deus cui obediare cuncta angelica creatura, quae tibi assistium dicentes: sanctus, sanctus, sanctus, dues fortis et immortalis, qui es, fuisti, et ciu in aeternum ... tu es ille dues qui dixisti ore tuo sanctissimo, petite et accipietis et dabitur vobis, Omnipotentiam tuam humiliter deprecor ut mittere digneris in hac nocte in somno Angelum tuum de cœlo, qui me regat omni tempore vitæ meæ, et instruat me circa illa quæ ad laudem et honorem tuum facturus sum, et quæ sum fugiturus pro salute animæ meæ, et illa quæ illi sum dicturus.... elogo clementiam tuam, o Domine Deus Rex Cœli et Terræ, ut cruas

---

[150] I.e. the person performing the ritual.

opprobrium et contemptium animæ meæ, ut sim purus ante conspectum tuum, et conspectum Angelorum tuorum, Amen."

When this prayer is finished, you should have the Sign of the Living God all ready and prepared, drawn on blessed paper, written with new and blessed ink and with a blessed feather pen from a Dove. After this, you should place the Sign of the Angel of the Day, as you can see below, and under the last Sign, you should write the item you wish to have.

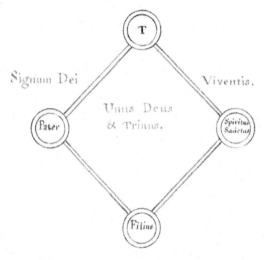

When you have done this, you should get up off your knees, holding the Signs we have mentioned in your hand and you should extinguish the candle and then place the Signs under your bed head and go to sleep quietly. When you are in your bed, you should devoutly recite your usual everyday prayers and at the end, you should add the prayer of the Angel of the Day, as you will see in due course and it is important for you to have learned it by heart, while always making sure that you have chosen the days ruled by the Angel, whose the mission corresponds to our request.

THE ANGEL FOR SATURDAY IS URIEL

And here is his Sign with his Character

Prayer of the Angel

Memento mei, Domine, qui ad similtudinem tuam creasti me, et dedisti mihi animam rationale ut cum Angelia intelligam, et in caritate tua maneam. Scio me esse indignum propteo mea scelera, et pavesco atque erubesco ante præsentiam tuam comparere; sed confisus misericordiæ tuæ ad tei veltio quasi Cervus ad fontem aquarum, ut mittere dignere Sanctum Angelum tuum Uriel, qui me doceat et instruat, atque dicat quid facturus sum, et quid evitare et fugere debeam.

Veni, Angele Dei, veni Uriel, et noli tardare, quia in te confido, in te spero per misericordiam Dei Creatoris tui et mei. Amen.

THE ANGEL FOR THURSDAY IS SALATIEL

And here is his Sign with his Character

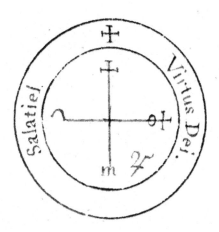

Prayer to the Angel

Memento mei, Domine, qui confregisti ora Draconum, et cæcitatem David qui prævaricavit in conspecta tuo, in summerando populum tuum, ad quem misisti Angelum tuum Salatiel de Cœlo, qui in ore gladii interfecit uno die quadraginta millia nomina, et misertus fuisti David servi tui plorantis, et misericordiam tuam potentia; ita et me famulum tuum et plorantem a te misericoriam petentem illuminare digneris per medium Angeli tui Salatiel, qui me custodiat, instruat, ne doceat secundum magnam misericordiam tuum. Amen.

THE ANGEL OF TUESDAY IS MICHAEL

And here is his Sign with his Character

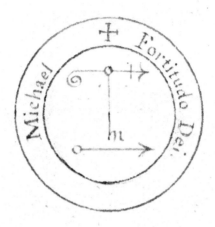

Prayer to the Angel

O Domine Deus omnipotens, in ejus manu sum omnia jura Regnorum, et quia est ille qui posit resistere voluntati tuæ ! Tu es ille de quo scriptum est : Sanctum et Terribile est Nomen ejus : Tu es ille in ejus manu sum Claves Regni Cœlorum et infernorum ; qui misisti Angelum tuum Michael pugnantem cum Dracone, et includentem et conculcantem eum in puteo inferni, sicut scriptum est perJohannem Apostolum in ejus Apocalysi, et calusi cum per annos mille. Ita te domine Deus humillime deprecor ut mittere digneris Angelum tuum Michael, qui cum manu valida sit fortitudo mea in omnibus meis negoteis peragendis pro salute animæ meæ, vel corporis mei. Per infinitam misericordiam tuam. Amen.

THE ANGEL OF SUNDAY IS RAPHAEL

And here is his Sign with his Character

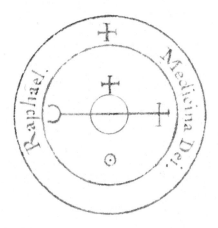

Prayer to the Angel

O Domine Deus omnipotens, qui Populum tuum fugientam de Ægypto deambulare fecisti per noctem illuminatam columna ignis ardentis, et per diem per nubem refrigerantem, et per medium maris rubri sicwis pedibus comitatum per Angelum tuum, et liberasti Tobiam filium Tobiæ de flumine, et a Demonus Sathanæ, revertentem incolumen ad patriam et domum suam, et cæcitatem batris sui illumasti, fac, exoro, ut videre valeani misericordiam tuam per medium Raphael Angeli tui me comitantis. Istam quæso, Domine Deus meus mitte Angelum tuum Raphael, qui me illuminet omnibus diebus vitæ meæ, et sit custos mei, et instruat at doceat me dormientem, per misericordiam tuam. Amen.

THE ANGEL OF FRIDAY IS ANATIEL

And here is his Sign with his Character

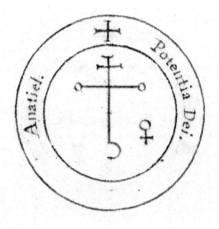

Prayer to the Angel

Memento mei Domine, qui dixisti ore tuo sanctissimo in quacumque hora petieritis aliquid a Patre meo dabitur vobis in nomine meo potentiam tuam precor ut mittere digneris in hac nocte Angelum tuum Sanctum Anatiel qui me instruat et doceat circa ea, quæ ad tui nominis gloriam sum facturus, ut fugiam omnes adversitates Satanæ, qui sicut Leo rugit ut devoret animam meam: Sed tu, O Domine misericors es ce omnipotens, et hanc gratiam mihi largiri potes. Veni, Angele Dei, et sis in comitalu meo, ita ut in tua presentia nullus inimicus mihi nocere valeat; Veni et noli tardare, quia in te confido et spero per misericordiam Dei Creatoris nostri. Amen.

The Angel Of Wednesday Is Adoniel

And here is his Sign with his Character

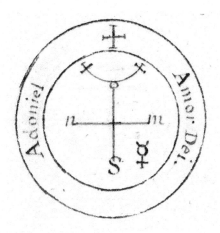

Prayer to the Angel

Memento mei, Domine, et miserere animæ meæ, sum misertur fuisti Abrahæ, qui servium voluntatem tuam postponendo paternum amorem erga Isaac, filium suum in monte illum offerebat in holocaustum omnipotentiæ tuæ et tu qui Pater omnium es, ei ab summam coritatem tuam et amorem tuum misisti Angelum tuum Adoniel de Cœlo dientem Abrahæ: diverte gladium tuum, quia Dominus tenuit te, et non pepercisti unio filio tuo propler me. Ita Domine Deus Cœli et Terræ Conditor mittere digneris Angelum tuum Adoniel de Cœlis, qui me instruat in mandatis tuis, et ostendat mihi fugere malum, et quærere bonum. Per misericordiam tuam. Amen.

THE ANGEL OF MONDAY IS GABRIEL

And here is his Sign with his Character

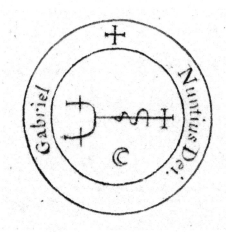

Prayer to the Angel

O Domine Deus omnipotens, qui pro salute generis humani misisti unicum filiam tuum de Cœlo, qui incaruatur est in ventre Beatæ Mariæ semper Virginis, mediante accessu tui Angeli Gabrielis proferentis voluntatem tuam, et annunciantem innaruationem filii tui Domini nostri Jesu Christi, qui natus est, et nuntiatus est Pastoribus rigitantionis semper gregem corum per medium Angelorum tuorum clamantium et dientium: Gloria in excelsis Deo, et in terra pax hominibus bonæ voluntatis. Ita rogo te, Domine Deus, ut mittere digneris Gabrielem Angelum tuum mihi nuntiantem voluntatem tuam pro salute animæ meæ, et quid facturus sum propter honorem meum. Per misericordiam tuam. Amen.

As soon as you have finished the Prayer of the Angel, as we have shown you above, you should strive to go to sleep peacefully and you should see some wonders and some magnificent things, just as the experiments have proven.

You should recognise, that after all this, this ritual is principally aimed at obtaining revelations for the things we wish to discover.

NB. It would be really useful to repeat the invitation to the Angel at the end of each prayer, as is written at the end of the first prayer and which begins with these words, *"Veni, Veni, &c"* and take care to change the name according to the day.

CONCERNING
MISCELLANEOUS CABALAH

4TH PART

This Part deals directly with Divination and it is also called *"The Book of Fate"*. It is said that it was compiled by Ghilon, an ancient Philosopher from Alexandria in Egypt and that for a long time after he had written it, it had been lost and hidden but it has finally been found again through revelation.

Take note that you should not request answers using this method, except in a case of necessity and when you do wish to make any request, you should do it on a bright day, untroubled by either wind, rain, or fog and you should make sure not to make any requests during any troubled day like this.

This Art has enjoyed a great reputation with the ancient Sages, who largely kept it a secret and when they did make use of it, they would begin by reciting the prayer below and then they would think of a number or they would even put their hand [randomly] over [a number in] the book and this number would give the reply they wished to have for the query they had made. These numbers number a hundred and twelve in total and each one of them contains a mystical response and you will need to examine the meaning of each word carefully. You can also perform this ritual for another person, who would like to ask a question for himself. When he has said the Prayer, he should chose one of the following numbers (not more than 112) by putting his hand on it, or he could even visualise one of the numbers in his mind's eye.

Prayer to God

"Lord of the Worlds, thou art God and thy name is Divine, thou art the God of Spirits and all flesh and Ruler over all the Regions from the Heights to the Depths, so that thou canst be found in all places and that thou art favourable towards those, who seek thee and pray to thee. I have come to present myself to thee with a contrite heart and a humble spirit in order to implore thy mercy and thy bounty, so that thou mayest permit me to know through this fate the true response of that, which I ask and I seek from thee. May the effects of thy clemency reach out over me and over the querent here present and mayest thou assist us in our query and mayest thou grant us thy potent help for the outcome of the response. For in thy hands alone lie power, steadfastness, counsel and prudence and we have no other salvation nor trust other than in thee and in thy law. And because our sins are the cause for the Prophesies to be removed from us and the reason why we have no more Prophets, neither any seer or rational person, nor any living voice, if it is not thy great and terrible name, it is why we have recourse to thee and make use of this Book of Fate, so that thou, who art the Lord of the World and of Fate, wilt permit us to know the truth, through this indulgence, which thou hast made in wishing to divide up the Land of Canaan, abundant in milk and honey and to divide it between thy people of Israel. Grant us, therefore, this favour, O God of Gods and Lord of Lords and may my prayer reach thy presence."

Then thou should pronounce these names:

Artimos, Vartimos, Carghilos, et in nomine Ledala, Delatam, Jelanan.

Here begin the 112 Responses:

1. Thou truly hast fears on this matter that thou hast presently been thinking about. But be assured, as that which thou askest, will come to thee with joy and honour. Thou hast in this request a joyful motive and good things will come of it and it will be granted to thee according to thy desires.

2. Behold a good omen and a fortunate time is foretold to gladden thee in this query. If thou fastest and prayest before this God who hast created it, he will grant thy wish. But strive to contain thy temptation, which is unrefined. And although thou mayest receive ill from men, however, do no evil, for great things will be granted to thee by Heaven. Place thy trust in the Lord God.

3. Angels of Mercy appease thee and speak to thy heart. Render thy graces to God, who hast given thee happiness. He will shine his radiance upon thee and he will swiftly give joy to thy soul, which thou desirest and thou wilt see thy wish fulfilled.

4. Remove thyself far from this matter, for it is not good for thee and thou wilt not be successful. Pray to God and commend thyself to him, he will not fail to honour thee, by which thou wilt be contained. And understand the matter well, so that shame will not

befall thee for the world to see and be careful that thy shame is not discovered.

5. Rise up, be quick and rejoice. For God hast provided all these good things for thee to foresee. This query foretelleth great gladness to come. For the planet is resplendent with joy and thou wilt enjoy a good reputation.

6. Joy and honour thou wilt have and much goodness will come to thee in a while. Fear nothing. For this trial, which thou experiencest, cometh from God, receive it gladly, for his ways are just and he will take pity upon thee.

7. It is for a good thing that thou hast given thyself pains to make this request and thy desire is good, God will give to thee that, which thou desirest. Trust in him and do only good. Humble thyself, that he may give thee what thou seekest.

8. Why, therefore, art thou boastful and dost speak improper words to thyself in thy heart? Thou desireest, thou thinkest and thou hopest that maybe they will be reconsolidated. To that, I say no! Wait, for it is better not to rush. Watch thyself and turn towards God, implore his mercy and maybe he will forgive thee. Therefore approach not this request and seek not for it, for there is neither happiness nor any advantage therein.

9. Glad tidings are foretold to thee. For the Planet is ascending and it lighteth thy way and the Angel maketh thee prosperous and happiness accompanieth thee. Trust God that thy question befiteth thee.

10. Son of man, behold, thou art looking amiss! Thy request hast nothing good in it, for it containeth too

much wickedness. Suffer by thyself and from it thou wilt receive a just reward from Heaven. And God will change the year to good for thee.

11. Son of man, all things cometh yet from God. But behold, thou sayest, "I will go and I will do such a thing." Go and withdraw into thyself and trust in God. For it is he who maketh men prosperous and he will grant thy request and all thy paths will be confounded and God will punish those who persecuteth thee.

12. This request demandeth pity. Rephrase it and be not stubborn thereof, for it is bad. Implore the bounty of God who comforteth thee and distanceth thee from this petition.

13. Know, O son of man, that a bad thought hast entered into thy spirit while making this request. For there is time and good will change into bad according to the hour and if thou seekest God's mercy, he will direct thy steps and will reward thee well and thou wilt find grace with him to thy advantage and at thy end. The wicked will cause thee grief and conceit from envy. But take care that maybe the names declared in the Name of the great and feared God will close in around thee.

14. My brother, I see that thou art saddened. Fear nothing, allow not the pain to enter deeper into thy heart, but reassure thyself against the schemes of the wicked, who will not be able to harm thee, no matter how much they seek to make thee stumble. Trust in God and stay not close to them. Do not allow them to penetrate into the secrets of thy heart. Do good to them, which will be as fire on their heads and thou wilt receive thy reward from God.

15. Fortunate art thou, who fearest God in this World, and considerest the idea that hast come to thee for thee to do. I hope that thou obtainest thy request and in this journey thou mayest go in peace, thou wilt return in peace and thou wilt approach with thy hands full and with a happy heart.

16. Know, my brother, that thy request hast been agreed and that goodness and happiness are being prepared for thee. Thou wilt see the goodness and thou wilt thereby rejoice.

17. That which thou prayest for is bad and how dost thy heart remain? Thou hast forgotten that it preventth thee from becoming prosperous and like thou sayest, *"I will go and I will do what I want"*, since it is not by strength that man overcometh calamities and evils. And may misfortune strike the man who dost not rely on God and who trusteth in men. For all is in the hands of God and there is only the fear of God, which is worthy. Humble thyself, therefore, and say not, *"I am mighty"*.

18. Son of man, thou hast not passed the tests and trials well, either through sickness or through bad reprimands. Thou hast forgotten everything, they have been the symbol of men, which thou hast consorted with, whose gloom thou hast not noticed. For if thou hadst been on thy guard, thou wouldst be better. Pay attention, therefore, for these men are wicked, for they seek harm for thee. Take care, and trust in God, who maybe will shatter the weft of their looms. They want to render evil for good.

19. Thou art faithful and thou walkest with honesty. Thou seeest thyself and thy request is just. Know, therefore,

that God is with thee and that many other people also love thee.

20. Trust in God, for thy request will be granted to thee with honour and if thou walkest on this path, God will rejoice in thee.

21. My brother, I see that thou trustest in God. It is why thy request will be granted with honour. Pursue always the same and God will assist thee.

22. Know that everything hath its hour and that the Angels foretell also what thou desireest as thou art favoured by God. Let us go, therefore into what thou requestest, for that will come to thee and after these days, God will make thee prosper. And take care not to trouble thyself too much with haste. For there is time for everything under the Heavens. And if thou proceedest to far in advance of thyself in this manner and without reflection, thou wilt stumble and thou wilt be ashamed and finally thou wilt have vengeance over thine enemies. Have courage that thou wilt have happiness in this matter. Pay close attention thereto.

23. My brother, God is all powerful, for he embraceth all. Why dost thou torment thy body and soul? If thou continuest in this fashion, thou wilt be lost. Reject from thy heart all of that and withdraw into thyself, for thou canst hope for nothing from this request: maybe at the end thy affairs will turn out well.

24. Know that it is better to be patient than powerful. For he who dominateth his will can do more than he who taketh cities. Thou hast done that which thou hast not wished to do and at present God hast already terminated thy request for thy wellbeing.

25. May God look upon thee with pity and he will make thee prosper and will send the Angels of Peace before thee and he will preserve thee from all evil. It is he, who hath settled thy request for thy good.

26. It is a moment of bounty, which hath been presented to thee, as well as good fortune. All thy steps and all thy wishes have been fulfilled and thy reputation will be increased to thy satisfaction.

27. Trust in God and distance thyself from wicked neighbours. Take courage and fear not the wicked, who will not be able to harm thee, if thou abstainest from consorting with them, for they know only evil. God will uphold thee and this will turn to thy advantage and will make thee forget all thy sorrows. May thy request be for good.

28. Thy request is sincere and true with no conceit and will bring thee peace, joy and a life free of sorrow, but as for the present, wait yet a while, for thou wilt not delay in receiving happiness. Pray to God and he will make thee contented.

29. Rejoice in the subject of thy request, for from now on, thou wilt have no more sorrow, nor tribulation and thank God, who hath preserved thee from death without thy knowing, but thou wilt soon know how. The matter hath been proven and it seems that thou hast not perceived it. But thy planet is ascending and is in a favourable aspect.

30. Believe not thy comrade at all and trust not thy superior, for this would be wise for thee. Be circumspect and guard thy silence. Know that all thy friends are false, they hate thee in secret and they carry envy for thee; they eat and they drink with thee

and they speak ill of thee. Avoid them, for God is with thee and he will save thee.

31. How many times hast thou given thyself pains for this request without having been able to achieve it? Because it is not yet the time and this is an occult matter. But God will draw the time near to it and will grant thee thy request for thy good and with honour and joy.

32. Take care and trouble not thyself, for thou canst not insist on this request, its time is not yet come and there is time for all. Endure a while longer and advise thyself with prudence and wait for God to console thee.

33. Trust in God and in a short while the fortunate moment will arrive, where heaven will grant thee that which thou desireest with success. A great reputation will come to thee and thou wilt have a golden necklace and bless God, who hath fulfilled thee.

34. Why art thou so proud and why dost thou boast about a matter that thou canst not do? Distance thyself from this request for this time for thou canst not succeed in it, for thy time hath not yet come. And even so, it will come to thee in part, abstain from it, for it will bring thee no advantage and its end will be evil.

35. It is certain and evident that thy request will be granted to thee with honour, joy and prosperity.

36. God is with thee and thy request hast been agreed. Thou wilt be consoled with it as thou wishest, that is why thou blesses the debt, with which he hath replied to thee.

37. Much grief and infirmity is ready to fall upon thee. Hasten to praise God, he will wait upon thee with a

shield and will make miracles to save thee. Trust in him, so that he will grant thy request in the end.

38. Thy request will be granted, for God is with thee.

39. Thou art running several projects in thy spirit. This request cometh only from God and if thou hadst rather wished for it, then thou wilt not receive it. But at present, be assured, that God is with thee and he will be thy succour.

40. The Angels of Peace come to meet thee in order to make thee prosper, for thy Planet favours thee. Thine enemies fall before thee, fear them not. Thy table will overflow with good things and thy treasures will fill thee up till thou art sated and thy request will be granted to thee.

41. The salvation of the Just cometh from God and say not, *"It is with my power and my skill that I have drawn myself out of this affair."* Praise God and although thou mayest be foolish, God will however carry out thy request and be prudent in thy life before he graspeth onto thee.

42. I have seen men who look for trouble for thee in secret. They eat and they drink with thee and plan evil against thee in their spirits. Fear not their wickedness, for God is with thee.

43. Why dost thou burden thyself? Cast this burden out of thy heart and know that if thou hast done everything and if thou hast removed thyself from this instead, thou wilt be presently relieved of this burden. Thou art being sought out, take care and pray to God.

44. The Heaven will extend much good and happiness over thee. Thou wilt receive prosperity and joy from this request. Be prepared to praise God with a sincere

heart and not half-heartedly and the outcome will be a happy one.

45. Thy request will be successful for thee and happiness will be brought to thee. Know, that thou wilt be renewed, that thine enemies will be confounded, that new favours and honours will be given to thee. Be not ashamed, nor debase thyself and bewilder thyself not, for great happiness will come to thee.

46. Think not on this request, which is not in thy power and will not succeed according to thy wishes. For I see that thou art full of hate, despising good morals and loving that, which is unjust. Forsake this path and walk on a righteous path and thou wilt foresee great riches and thou wilt no longer have need of anyone, although thou wither from indecent things, pay attention to it and work with the fear of God and thou wilt prosper in that which thou doest.

47. I see that thou hast been given bad advice and that they have cast upon thee many things, which make thee afraid, distance these fears from thy heart, trust in God and believe not in the words of these men who seek to harm thee and God will be with thee.

48. Glad tidings in all things from God I foretell thee. For he hath looked upon thee with a merciful eye and he will give thee the strength and the power and he will command his Angels to watch over thee and to protect thee in all of thy ways. And this request seemeth hard in thy heart and thou hast fears thereof. But fear nothing, for he will grant it to thee with joy.

49. Be not saddened by thy request, for thou wilt be assisted and thou wilt prosper in this. And thou must not grieve thyself, for God hast granted thee much

good and although thy wishes come a little late, be not anxious, take heart, be firm and all good things will not fail to come to thee.

50. Let it go. For thou dost not know the commandments of God and although God may be slow, he is however satisfied at the end.

51. Son of man, fear God, abstain for evil and do good. Behave not with half a heart and tempt not God, for that which thou requestest is not fitting for thee and it is wrong. Let it go and seek a just request and if thou repentest, it will be good for thee, if not, thou wilt see.

52. Say not, *"I will go and I will do what I want."* For thou wilt not be able to do it and thou wilt not succeed. This request is not good, it would be better for thee to abandon it.

53. It is fitting that thy request be done quickly, for thou wilt have perfect success thereof, because thou hast fear of God. Work, therefore, with courage and with trust, thou wilt prosper, thy goal is good.

54. Know that God is thy succour and he will make thee prosper. Be assured, that thy request will be accorded to thee, for the Angels of Peace will come to direct thy steps.

55. I advise thee not to give thyself any worries, nor to torment thyself. For this request, thou hast formerly given thyself worries on its account, without ever having been able to succeed. Be not in such a hurry, so that thou rushest not against any obstacles. For the time is not yet come to find it. A veil coverth it until it is time for thee to find it and thou wilt have much happiness.

56. A great thing thou askest, and thou hast fears thereof, but fear nothing, since there is no anger in what thou hast in thy heart and thou fearest God. Pray to God, that he will fulfil thy wishes.

57. I foretell glad tidings, seeing that thy request is good. There is nothing in it is that is displeasing. I see that thou fearest for the Vessel that is at sea, it may not suffer much, but that will not be for long, it will come back to thee in peace.

58. Boast not in saying that thou wilt succeed in thy requisition, since as the lie is in thy soul, seek it no longer, as thou wilt find nothing.

59. Thou must not begrudge thy comrade, for at the end thou wilt repent of it and that will serve for nothing.

60. Forsake this request. For another is doing it all the same and wisheth thee to fall into a trap. Also, desist from this and seek it not.

61. Happiness, peace and good things are ready to come to thee through this request, which will be accompanied by gladness.

62. Give praise to the living and eternal God, humble thyself before him with a contrite heart and when thou quitest these bad deeds, thou wilt then be satisfied.

63. Why dost thou grieve over this? Its time is not yet come and its keys have not yet been consigned. Torment not thyself in vain. Fast and pray to God.

64. Be not impious, for thou diest before thy time, guard thyself that thou dost not speak any more falsehoods, for thy tongue will go to judgement first and will repair that which thou hast spoiled and God will satisfy thee.

65. Rejoice for thyself, for thy request will be accorded to thee, for it is a happy moment in thy dwellings.

66. I see that men hate thee and that they say evil of thee and thou hast also some quarrels with others. Fear God and say not to them that God will confound them. God will know how to make thee prosper in all things that thou requestest.

67. Moved by a happy inspiration, thou hast made thy request at a good moment and thou hast come to me. Thy request will be granted and thou wilt prosper in thy ways, if thou wilt follow it instead. Delay not, therefore.

68. If thou listenest to my advice, thy heart will be disposed towards God, thou wilt yet endure, thou wilt allow a few days to pass and thou wilt obtain it.

69. Thy request is proper, be not discouraged and debase not thyself, for God is with thee and thou wilt have happiness.

70. Know that this request hath come to thy spirit at a good moment. It will be accorded to thee by Heaven, for thou hast suffered enough. Thou wilt find grace and mercy and thou wilt forget all thy sorrows.

71. I foretell thee yet more glad tidings; be not saddened, raise thyself up and go to the ends of the world, for God is with thee.

72. Give not thyself too many concerns, for thou wilt not have that which thou hast requested. Thou dost not have prudence, but pain in thy interior, not having any good morals. Thus, think not thereon and strive to trust in God, who at the end will come to console thee.

73. Be not hasty, for thou wilt not achieve success in this. Avoid quarrels, which only serve to separate thee

from the affection of the world, even more so because thou art deceitful and thou wilt not walk on the path of righteous. Thus, give not thyself sorrow in vain. Wait and control thy steps better.

74. Know that all cometh from God and man can take nothing with his hands. He will give himself much restlessness and sorrow and will succeed in nothing. But God hast everything in his power. Thus be patient and wait yet, for a happy moment will come in a short while and thou wilt then be content.

75. Abstain from this request, for it is not good and hath only vanity and that which thou hast spoken, will not withstand thee. Believe not in the man who reporteth everything and pay attention to what we have told thee.

76. Rejoice in thyself, that the hour of gladness cometh to favour this request, for thy fate and thy well-being come together to save thee and to make thee content in a short while.

77. Thou art foretold that glad tidings await thee and that the Angels come to meet thee and that thy requests have already been granted, as thou wilt soon see.

78. I see that thou hast endured many sorrows, adversities and misery and that thou seekest this mystery, but thou canst not have it, because thy request is distant and placeth thy person in suspension. Seek it not, for things are not all equal and if time passeth, it will come to pass for thee with satisfaction.

79. Distance thyself from these evils and from this thing that thou hast in thy head, because it is not good and will not give thee happiness. Take guard not to fall

into ignominy and blush with shame. But I foretell thee that this or another thing that is well disposed towards thee, is good for thee.

80. With joy, thou wilt be given that which thou requestest, it being already thus disposed in Heaven. Be firm and seek with courage and thou wilt succeed to thy advantage and contentment.

81. God will make thy steps prosper and will grant thee thy request. It hath already been fulfilled. It will be well to forsake it, take another from it, which will be well for thee.

82. Much goodness and many kinds of grain will come to thee. Thou must praise and give thanks to God, who granteth thee joy. Pursue, therefore, without delay, so that thou wilt have much contentment.

83. Go not to seek the ways of God and tempt him not, so that thou dost not risk to stumble and if these days come to pass, return to me, I will tell thee what thou art to do.

84. Trust in God and pray to him and go not to pray to men, nor trust in them. Thou art wise and prudent, it would be foolhardy to trust in ingrates and in liars. Thou must consider well what this request demandeth from knowledge, from fear and even from contemplation.

85. The moment is most propitious for that which thou desirest, thou mayest take a woman; thou mayest go and do all things, while imploring clemency and assistance from God, who sendeth his Angels to aid thee in their ministry.

86. Thou must gird thy loins as a man and make thy request and thou wilt have the contentment that thou

desireest and seek the honour of God with trust, for thy prayer hast already been fulfilled.

87. Thou hast in thy spirit many things to ask concerning thy fate. Thy way of living is tenacious. Thou sayest that thy hope is lost and thou waitest, thinking that thy days have passed in vain. But be not saddened, for thy pleasure is vague and thy hopes are well endorsed, although the time hath not yet arrived and although thou sayest that everything is a futile and misguided chore, know that everything cometh from God and trust in him, so that thou mayest have thy reward from him.

88. Fear nothing from these evildoers, who rise up against thee to harm thee and pretend to be thy friends. For God will make them fall to their feet, because these are false men and thou wouldst be most foolish to listen to what they say and to revel to them thy secrets. Thy fate is great and fortunate, it is because they wish to make thee fall, but it will be them who will fall.

89. Stay in thy house and thou wilt be respected and go not to consort with vile men, for thy nourishment cometh from God. Thus, tire thyself not to make these journeys, nor give thyself sorrows for children. For God will give thee riches, children, and that which thou desirest. Implore, therefore, his clemency and delay not in rejoicing.

90. Do not make too many vows, for several times thou hast made them to God and thou hast not kept them. There is nothing forgotten before God, thus keep always thy promises to God and he will look upon thee with sympathy.

91. Be not so foolhardy to look for an occult thing and give not thyself over to it in vain. God knoweth where things are and how well thou understandest these secrets. There is therefore nothing given to the hands of man, for he runneth too many projects in his head and is subject to error.

92. Who can know what will come of man, as he seeth himself as fish and birds ensnared in nets? He doth not know the hour of his death and occult things are known only by the Eternal and by the man who feareth God.

93. Often thou hast wanted to do penitence and thou hast never done it. Presently will come days of calamity, filled with fear and thou wilt have recourse to God. Be calm, he hath already commanded good things in order to fulfil thy request, for thou lovest the Lord.

94. Since thou hast only good thoughts for thyself and for thy neighbour, no evil will befall thee and in a short while, thy request will be granted. Thou wilt be envied by many who seek to annul thy request, but God will not heed them and will soon grant thee contentment.

95. Thou canst not prevent death. Stay not in the abodes of great men. Run not after honours and dignities, for the time for that hath not yet arrived.

96. How dost thou have so much confidence to claim this? Pay attention, for the many times that thou hast had such confidence, thou hast run into danger, from which God hast saved thee. Turn to God and wait, for he will have pity on thee.

97. How God will bestow kindness upon thee, if thou wishest to pay attention! Thy request will be granted

and this enemy who wisheth to bring thee down so that he can be in thy place, he will not succeed in it. Fear him not, as soon as thou loveest God.

98. Thou thinkest it well to rejoice that thou hast escaped from the grave and that thy days have been renewed. Thou wilt pass them in joy, thou wilt have children, whose little one will become a great one. He will console thee and relieve thee in thy works and from thy sorrows.

99. Thou hast done a foolish thing, since thou wast worthy to have good things and thou wast in a hurry to do evil and in so doing, thou hast fallen down. It is not enough that thou hast done this, for still thou seekest to pursue it. But watch thy soul, for thou dost not know the judgments of God who giveth birth to the day and who will send thee evil if thou continuest to be so impious.

100. Thou dost not know that the aim of thy request leaneth towards evil and that several persons, like thyself, have sought the same thing and have fallen. It would be better for thee to study thy request a little more in order to obtain it and address thyself to God.

101. The merit which thou hast received is eternal. Fear nothing, work and do what thou desirest, for thy request will be granted to thee and thou wilt be honoured by many people.

102. Since thou believest in God, trust in him, for he will make thine enemies fall and he will fulfil thy requests to thy great satisfaction.

103. Woe to thee, if thou dost not do good towards God. Forsake all evil and trust in him, for he will fulfil the wishes of thy heart.

104.Distance thyself not from the fear of God, so that thou wilt not be hated by thy friends. Avoid doing evil and God alone can save thee.

105.Be blessed by God, as Abraham our father hath been, and God will be with thee to give thee a good reputation, he will bless thee and will fulfil thy request.

106.Since thou hast inclined thy soul to the fear of God, thou wilt have all power over men and over nations, for thou art pleasing to God, who will fulfil thy request.

107.Thou art small and insignificant and lookest like thou art boastful without thinking about what thou art today and that tomorrow thou wilt be no longer. Man doth not remain the same and after his end, he will be cast away like a dead beast. Turn to God and he will have pity on thee.

108.What wilt thou be doing on the day that God cometh to visit thee? Strive to give justice and maybe he will calm his fury, for he doth not want thy ruin and will be able to grant thy request.

109.Yesterday, thou hast anticipated thy prayer. Thou hast made thy voice heard and thou hast thereby made thy judgment favourable and thou wilt be written in the Book of Life because of it and thou hast inherited the good things of this world as the heritage of Jacob.

110.God will increase thy honour, for thy goal is good and he will prosper greatly at the end, like Jacob our father and thou wilt see all that thou desirest.

111.Poor creature, why dost thou seek a thing that thou canst not do? Carry no envy against thy brother, because he is bigger than thyself and thou wilt have need of him and then thy request will be granted to thee.

112. Trouble not thyself, and be not discouraged from that, on which thou hast worked greatly without having been able to succeed. For the time of strife will pass and thou wilt be delivered and thou wilt find that which thou seekest.

END

Note that when you want to have an answer, instead of thinking about one of these 112 numbers, you can also use a fixed circle on a solid base which has a pivot in the middle holding up a spinning dial, which will point to one of these 112 numbers, which will be marked around the circumference of the circle.

You can also use a deck of blank cards and on each of them you will have marked one of the 112 numbers and even the answer, if you wish. Mix the cards well and then cut the deck and pull one out from the middle of the deck, which will give you the answer you are seeking.[151]

---

[151] Alternatively you could use the Minor Arcana of the Tarot, with each card having two values as upright or reversed, giving 112 = 2 x 56 possible interpretations.

SELECTED BIBLIOGRAPHY

Agrippa, H. C.; *Fourth Book of Occult Philosophy*; 2005; Ibis Press/Nicolas-Hays; Berwick

-----------; *Three Books of Occult Philosophy*; 1993; Llewellyn; St Paul

Betz, Hans Dieter (ed); *The Greek Magical Papyri in Translation*; 1992; University of Chicago Press; Chicago

Butler, E.M.; *Ritual Magic*; 1979; Cambridge University Press; Cambridge

Daiches, Samuel; *Babylonian Oil Magic in the Talmud and in the later Jewish Literature*; 1913; Jews College; London

De Givry, Emile Grillot; *Illustrated Anthology of Sorcery, Magic and Alchemy*; 1991; Zachary Kwintner; London

D'Este, Sorita,& Rankine, David; *Wicca: Magickal Beginnings*; 2008; Avalonia; London

Eamon, William; *Science and the Secrets of Nature: Books of Secrets in Medieval and Early Modern Culture*; 1994; Princeton University Press; Princeton

Fanger, Claire (ed); *Conjuring Spirits: Texts and Traditions of Medieval Ritual Magic*; 1998; Sutton Publishing Ltd; Stroud

Kiesel, William (ed); *Picatrix: Ghayat Al-Hakim*; 2002; Ouroboros Press; Seattle

King, B.J.H. (trans); *The Grimoire of Pope Honorius III*; 1984; Sut Anubis Books; Northampton

Peterson, Joseph (ed); *The Sixth and Seventh Books of Moses*; 2008; Ibis Press; Florida

---------- (ed, trans); *Grimorium Verum*; 2007; CreateSpace Publishing; California

Rohrbacher-Sticker, Claudia; *A Hebrew Manuscript of Clavicula Salomonis*, Part II; 1995; in *British Library Journal*, 21:128-136.

----------; *Mafteah Shelomoh: A New Acquisition of the The Key of Solomon*; 1993/94; in *Jewish Studies Quarterly*, Volume 1. 3:263-270

Scot, Reginald; *Discoverie of Witchcraft*; 1886 (reprint of 1665 edition); Elliot Stock, London

Shah, Sayed Idries; *The Secret Lore of Magic*; 1957; Frederick Muller Ltd; London

Skinner, Stephen & Rankine, David; *The Veritable Key of Solomon*; 2008; Golden Hoard Press, Singpaore

----------; *The Goetia of Dr Rudd*; 2007; Golden Hoard Press; Singapore

----------; *The Keys to the Gateway of Magic*; 2005; Golden Hoard Press; Singapore

Thompson, C.J.S.; *Mysteries and Secrets of Magic*; 1927; John Lane; London

Trachtenberg, Joshua; *Jewish Magic and Superstition*; 2004; University of Pennsylvania; Pennsylvania

Waite, A.E. (writing as 'Grand Orient'); *Complete Manual of Occult Divination: The Book of Destiny* (2 volumes); 1972; University Books Inc; New York

INDEX

CPSIA information can be obtained at www.ICGtesting.com
Printed in the USA
BVOW06s1118011215

428780BV00017B/64/P